GROUP LEADERSHIP TRAINING AND SUPERVISION MANUAL

for
**Adolescent Group Counseling
In Schools**

3rd Edition

Fred Jay Krieg, Ph.D.
Clinical Psychologist

ACCELERATED DEVELOPMENT INC.
Publishers
Muncie   Indiana

GROUP LEADERSHIP TRAINING AND SUPERVISION MANUAL
for
Adolescent Group Counseling in Schools

3rd Edition

Library of Congress Number: 88-70010

International Standard Book Number: 0-915202-80-8

PRINTED IN THE UNITED STATES OF AMERICA

Technical Development: Virginia Cooper
          Tanya Dalton
          Marguerite Mader
          Sheila Sheward

ACCELERATED DEVELOPMENT Inc., PUBLISHERS
3400 Kilgore Avenue, Muncie, Indiana 47304
(317) 284-7511

ACKNOWLEDGEMENT

ADOLESCENT GROUP COUNSELING IN SCHOOLS is the outgrowth of my experiences in leading groups in my private practice and as Treatment Coordinator of the Adolescent Mental Health Unit, St. Joseph's Hospital, Parkersburg, West Virginia. It is the result of extensive research and a belief that adolescents are best served in the school by counseling sessions which function more like inpatient than outpatient groups.

When the Adolescent Unit opened January 5, 1981, and I began to lead groups, I realized that I had not led one since graduate school. However, that group consisted of fellow graduate students; a most unrealistic membership. I was soon to learn adolescent groups are not that easy. Later, after extensive reading, countless continuing education courses, and some one thousand groups, I wrote the preliminary edition to this training and supervision manual in the summer of 1985.

Through the cooperation and support of the Pleasants County School system, I had the opportunity to apply theory to practice. The training manual was used by the "magnificant seven" (the group leaders in the first year of the project) and the Pleasants County Schools to develop the ***Adolescent Group Counseling in Schools*** program that became known as the "Pleasants County Project". This third edition represents three years of progress and refinement of that program as well as the information gathered from the growth of the project to other school districts. The experiences, insights, and results of those programs have been incorporated in this edition in the hope that students in other school systems might benefit from these learnings.

The Group Leadership Training and Supervision Manual is designed to teach group leadership skills to school counselors, specialists, and classroom teachers who serve as group leaders in the program. It was developed with extensive help from Diane Braun, Guidance Counselor, and Project Coordinator. I would also like to thank the staff of the Pleasants County Middle School, Mrs. Donna Pratt Barksdale, Principal. Without their ongoing support, encouragement, and assistance, the project would have never been so successful. Gratefully, acknowledgements are extended to my colleagues and co-leaders on the Adolescent Mental Health Unit who got me started in this project, John Fitzpatrick, Eldon Frank, Vic Carlson, and most importantly, Rick Stanley. Their openness and willingness to share ideas, methods, and techniques have stimulated my thinking and represent a major contribution to this work. My deepest gratitude to Christine Simpson, Supervisor for the Bangor Area School District project, for her assistance in writing the introduction to this manual. Her tremendous commitment to the project and clear writing style have added greatly to the effectiveness of that program and to the manual. One would be at a loss to not thank Jerri Caplinger for editorial assistance in the rewriting of this third edition, and Richard L. Rogers for administrative support in project management. My father designed and produced the cover, and I am most appreciative. Thanks also goes to Bettie Lewis, Kathy Gabler, and Linda Hinzman who patiently typed innumerable revisions with helpful comments. Finally, I would like to thank my wife Sallie, and my sons Joshua and Zachary, for their love and being the kind of family that allows me to write. Last, and most importantly, I wish to acknowledge my debt to the many adolescents who volunteered to participate in this project and from whom we all learned so much. For their help, we are forever grateful.

Fred Jay Krieg, Ph.D.
Winter 1988

CONTENTS

PART ONE   TRAINING PROGRAM OUTLINE

PART TWO SAMPLE MATERIALS

PART THREE SUPERVISION

LIST OF FIGURES

GROUP LEADERSHIP
TRAINING
AND
SUPERVISION

for
Adolescent
Group Counseling
in Schools

INTRODUCTION

Most parents and school officials realize children need more than academics to be successful. The unrelenting pressures of growing up in today's world have created a crisis in adolescent adjustment. Problems are many and varied: high school dropout rates, suicide, substance abuse, teen pregnancies, delinquency, vandalism, divorce, and depression. But beyond these identified issues, the difficulties posed by the adolescent years are characterized by a lack of intimacy and involvement. How are these students to meet these needs? With student/counselor rates in excess of 350/1, to expect school counselors to accomplish this task is unrealistic.

After working thirteen years in private practice, including five years treating hospitalized adolescents, I have observed the power of group in helping adolescents understand their behavior and cope with the stresses of life. Many hospitalizations could have been prevented if adolescents had the communication skills and a place to air their feelings. Group provided the ideal vehicle to accomplish that goal and my desire was to make group available in the educational setting. The **Adolescent Group Counseling in Schools** project and the **Group Leadership Training and Supervision Manual** is the culmination of my dream to develop a primary prevention program within the school environment.

Rather than tailor counseling services for one target population or problem, the program is designed to broach fundamental issues of self-esteem, peer pressure, decision-making, alienation, and interpersonal skills. All students, regardless of their specific status, participate. The goal is to reach a greater number of students and empower them with the ability to act and react more responsibly in their personal lives. The focus is prevention, not crisis intervention or treatment.

The Pleasants County Project in West Virginia and subsequent successes proved that school personnel can be trained to lead groups effectively and achieve astounding results. Acceptance of the program has resulted in its continued expansion, not only within West Virginia but to other states as well. Counselors feel an immediate increase in their effectiveness, teachers feel they become better teachers, principals can see positive changes in student behavior and that the school climate is positively enhanced, and parents voice appreciation for the added attention their children receive. More importantly, students indicate that group makes a significant difference in their attitude toward school, parents, teachers, and friends. They told the value of group. The project resulted in dramatic improvements in student behavior. Withdrawn students became more interactive and aggressive students demonstrated better controls. Overall, students exhibited increased academic performance, better citizenship, and a pronounced improvement in self esteem.

Adolescent Group Counseling In Schools is a proven primary prevention program which takes advantage of the heightened significance of peer interaction during the adolescent period and which capitalizes on the unique setting that the school provides.

For *The Group Leadership Training and Supervision Manual* to be meaningful, one needs to understand *The Adolescent Group Counseling in Schools Program.* It is a generic group counseling program for adolescents in grades five through twelve. The groups are based upon the theoretical position that school groups are a subsystem of the school itself. A grave error would be made if one was to perceive the adolescent's behavior in group as solely determined by personal dynamics and to ignore the influence the school setting has on facilitating and/or inhibiting the expression of feelings and actions. The effectiveness of this program demonstrates that school counseling groups function more like inpatient groups than outpatient groups because the group reflects and is intensified by the dynamic process of the school, having a richness of data to draw from that is not readily available to classic outpatient groups.

Each group consists of eight to ten adolescents and two group leaders. A careful balance, which represents a cross-section of the student population, is deemed critical to the formation of the groups. Adolescents are chosen with regard to their levels of achievement, verbalization, adjustment, and high academic/low academic, vocal/non-vocal, well-adjusted/behaviorally problematic, and extraverted/introverted students in order to recreate a miniature of the school environment.

Students attend group on a given hour and day of the week during a regularly scheduled class period for the entire year. Once group sessions begin in early October, no students are permitted to leave group and no new students are added. Students recognize their commitment for the full academic year and attend thirty group sessions. By maintaining the group's integrity, group cohesiveness and mutual trust, salient forces in the counseling process, are fostered.

Group leaders are volunteers from the faculty, including school psychologists, counselors, and teachers. In addition, a building coordinator for every school and a program supervisor for the particular school system are identified to assist with the technical and professional aspects of the project. Following intense training sessions (the manual provides the basis of this training), the staff is assigned primary and secondary leadership functions. To provide continuing skill development, ongoing monthly supervision of the group leaders becomes an integral factor of the program.

Structure is provided by the group leaders, but no planned activities or lessons are provided. Students are encouraged to focus on thoughts and feelings, troublesome life situations, and other concerns group members may express. Within the confidential group setting, students have a forum to discuss problems and social issues not appropriately aired in the classroom. Topics originated by group members include academic pressures, personal inadequacies, family concerns, substance abuse, suicide, rejection, peer pressure, and relationships.

A major benefit of the program stems for the issue of "universality" whereby the adolescents learn, perhaps for the first time, that they are not alone in their particular feelings or circumstances. This bond of commonality helps to lessen thoughts of alienation and isolation and to foster a sense of belonging. Futher advantages of the counseling focus on students receiving honest, undeniable feedback from group members—peers who know each other's "true form" outside of the groups. Learning the effect and impact of their behavior from other students assumes greater potency than receiving the identical message from an adult, underscoring the strength of the adolescent group counseling program. Finally, the group sessions provide a safe environment in which to forge and practice new skills, including honesty and behavior change.

To be effective, the group project must become an administrative priority among building principals whose support for its implementation and eventual success is critical. In particular, the concept of "sacred group hour" must be endorsed by the administration whereby teachers are requested not to schedule tests, field trips, assemblies or similar activities that would interfere with the group. Moreover, in some instances, students are released from academic subjects to attend group (although the majority of pupils are excused from study halls, art classes, etc.), requiring teacher cooperation for makeup work or attendance in an alternate class.

UNIQUENESS OF PROGRAM

The *Adolescent Group Counseling in Schools* model varies from many group counseling programs in several highly significant and unique ways.

First, the project is viewed as a generic, primary prevention program designed for all students. Student selection, in addition to assessing levels of achievement, adjustment, verbalization and socialization, focuses on three primary populations: (1) "model" students (class representatives, star athletes, "natural" leaders), (2) "issue" students (those facing concerns such as substance abuse, suicide, divorce, and (3) "problem" students (those exhibiting delinquent behavior, truants or discipline problems.

The inclusion of model adolescent is a key component of the program. It is through these youth that the group counseling program derives a high sense of credibility and acceptance. Issue and problem youth are generally awaren when they are being solely targeted, yet again, for special programs or disciplinary measures. However, the involvement of model peers signals something unique about the counseling project, helping to reduce the initial resistance and defensiveness often generated by issue or problem adolescents.

Apart from lending credibility to the program, the inclusion of model students is appropriate when considering the objectives of the primary prevention project, namely, increased self esteem, greater self responsibility, and improved interpersonal skills. With these project goals, it is evident that all students can benefit from the thrust of the counseling program. Likewise, it is deemed favorable for positive role models to be inclined as group members.

A second critical difference between *The Adolescent Group Counseling in Schools* program and a more typical counseling undertaking is the use of teachers as group leaders in addition to psychologists and counselors. By redirecting the duties and responsibilities of faculty members, a significantly greater percentage of the student population is served without the need for staff expansion. Utilizing teachers as an integral part of the program enhances credibility among the faculty and students. Teachers make excellent group leaders as they are comfortable working with small groups and enjoy the challenge of expanding their skills. Teachers often comment that the program opens their eyes and helps them be more patient and understanding with students.

The program is designed to expand in a geometric progression, the third distinctive feature. In subsequent years of the project, all secondary leaders move into leadership positions with new personnel trained for secondary leadership roles. Consequently, the number of groups formed, and students served, can double annually. Expansion of the program can continue, without the need to hire additional staff, until the determination is made that the project is at a size optimum for the school. The goal is to offer the group experience to all students at least once during each of their elementary/junior/senior high passages.

A fourth critical difference of the model focuses on scheduling the weekly group session for the entire school year. Fundamental to this approach is the realization that groups progress through predictable, developmental stages which collectively benefit from a longer time span in order to attain maximum therapeutic value. The school calendar is well suited to the progression of groups through the distrust and integration phases into the working stage where change actually is generated. Short-term counseling work or premature termination of group members threaten to eclipse the core of the working phase of the group process. For these reasons, students make a commitment for the entire year. Consequently, the potential for change is maximized by allowing the natural operation of groups to unfold without time restraints.

The fifth and perhaps the most significant component of the *Adolescent Group Counseling in Schools* program is the ongoing, monthly supervision of all group leaders. The supervision program (detailed in the last portion of the manual) enables the group leader to grow as the group is developing, so that when the group is ready to deal with important issues, the group leader is competent to cope with even the most difficult of group situations. Initial training, coupled with follow-up supervision, is vital for the development of effective group leadership skills and affords a greater degree of comfort for the staff.

All group counseling sessions are videotaped and form the basis of the monthly supervisory meetings. This essential peer supervision is designed to improve competencies, to share common problems, and to offer support. Moreover, as the groups progress through their developmental stages, the monthly meetings provide specific, comprehensive training for the next phase of the group counseling process.

The videotapes are accessible only to the supervisor and the group leaders through the forum of supervision, and are erased following each monthly meeting. By the end of the year, no permanent record exists of the group sessions. Confidentiality is deemed a critical component of the program to be upheld by members and leaders. Students, after the initial weeks, do not regard the videotaping as intrusive or threatening, realizing the purpose of and highly limited access to the tapes. The cooperation and support of the administration allows the issue of confidentiality to remain inviolate as principals realize that, even to them, the content of group is inaccessible.

Therapeutic intervention for adolescents can be successful in the school environment. The increased need and demand to expand student counseling without dramatically increasing the number of professional staff requires an innovative approach. The **Group Leadership Training and Supervisory Manual** provides a system and the needed information that enables schools to bring group counseling services to virtually all students by addressing their fundamental needs and equipping adolescnets with skills and self-understanding to better cope with the multitude of stresses they face.

PROJECT OVERVIEW

I. A generic group counseling program for students grades 5 through 12

    A. Teacher led

        1. Leader

        2. Co-leader

    B. 8 to 10 students in each heterogeneous group (3 to 5 groups per school in the initial year)

    C. Group meets once per week for one class period throughout the entire school year for a total of at least 30 weeks

    D. Designed to expand in geometric progression so that eventually every student can be served

    E. Group structure is provided through skills taught to leaders (No planned activities or topics)

II. Primary prevention program which addresses significant problems in education today: high-risk, teen suicide, drug & alcohol abuse, teen pregnancy, delinquency, and vandalism.

    A. Primary goals

        1. Improve self-concept

        2. Increase self-responsibility

        3. Improve interpersonal skills

    B. Proven intervention strategy

        1. Takes advantage of peer interaction during the adolescent period

        2. Takes advantage of the unique setting that the school provides

        3. Provides a vehicle for students to discuss problems and social issues not appropriately aired in the classroom

III. Organizational Structure

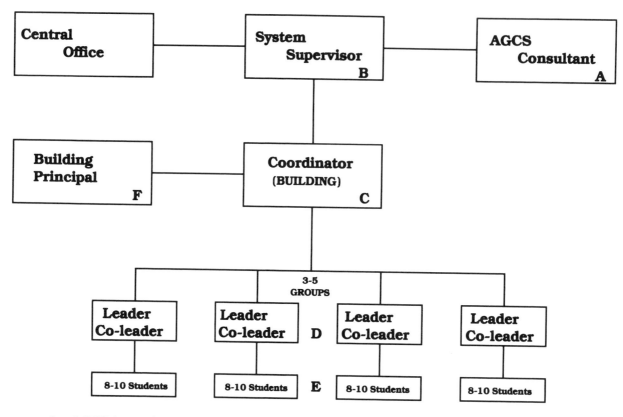

A. **AGCS (American Group Counseling Services) Consultant**

A mental health professional skilled in adolescent group counseling

B. **System Supervisor**

Person administratively responsible for the implementation of group counseling in the school system

C. **Coordinator** (1 per building)

A guidance counselor or school psychologist in each building responsible for program management and implementation

D. **Leaders and Co-Leaders**

Counselors, specialists and classroom teachers to serve as group leaders and co-leaders

E. **Students**

A cross-section of the school population including model students, problem students, and students with significant issues. These students are verbal, non-verbal, achievers, underachievers, socialized and undersocialized

F. **Building Principal**

Support and commitment essential to program success

IV. The AGCS System

A. Beginning in Spring

   1. Preliminary planning and organization

   2. Identification of staff for participation

   3. Obtain community support and cooperation

   4. Student selection

   5. Planning program evaluation (Pre & Post)

B. Summer

   1. Staff Training

      a. 18 to 30 staff members can be trained

      b. Graduate credit can be arranged

      c. Group Leadership Skills (2 days)

      d. Third day of training is optional and can be in any education/prevention area

         (1) alcohol and drug education/prevention

         (2) high-risk students

         (3) suicide

         (4) teen pregnancy

         (5) drop-out prevention

C. September

   1. Project Awareness Day

      a. Meeting of project staff and school administration

      b. Student assemblies

      c. Faculty staff meeting

      d. Parent night

         (1) overview of adolescent issues

         (2) overview of group counseling program

         (3) question and answer session

2. Coordinators Meeting (½ day)

    a. Organization meeting

    b. Student selection

    c. Individual interviews

    d. Evaluation and planning

3. Beginning of regularly scheduled meetings with AGCS Consultant (1 day)

    a. Individual interviews

    b. Teach RAPP

D. October

  1. Groups begin

  2. Supervision (1 day)

    a. Review RAPP

    b. Teach **Distrust** Stage

E. November

  1. Supervision (1 day)

    a. Review Distrust Stage

    b. Teach **Integration** Stage

F. December

  1. Supervision (1 day)

    a. Review Integration Stage

    b. Teach **Christmas** Activity

G. January

  1. Supervision (1 day)

    a. Review Christmas Activity

    b. Teach **Working** Stage

H. February

    1. Coordinators meeting (1/2 day)

I. March

    1. Supervision (1 day)

        a. Review Working Stage

        b. Discuss individual cases

J. April

    1. Coordinators meeting (1/2 day)

        a. Plan program expansion for next school year

        b. Discuss evaluation data gathering process

K. May

    1. Supervision

        a. Review program outcomes

        b. Teach *Termination* Stage

        c. Evaluate program success

    2. Project Review Day

        a. Student assemblies

        b. Parent night

            (1) review program outcomes

            (2) discuss plans for next year

PART ONE

TRAINING PROGRAM OUTLINE

I

RATIONALE FOR GROUP
COUNSELING IN SCHOOLS

A. SCHOOL PROVIDES UNIQUE SETTING

1. Most sustained contact outside primary family

    a. Develop loyalty and intimacy beyond immediate family

    b. Schools as "second parent"

2. Importance of peer pressure during adolescent period

3. Important place for social contact

4. Groups utilize adolescent's excessive sensitivity to school events

B. BENEFITS FOR SCHOOLS

1. Addresses significant problems in public education

    a. Recent Commission reports and public opinion polls

        (1) Increase in violence

        (2) Increase in destruction of property

        (3) Increase in drop-out rate

        (4) Decrease in school attendance

        (5) Decline in achievement

    b. Schools are being asked to address significant social issues

        (1) High-risk

        (2) Suicide

        (3) Teen pregnancy

        (4) Drug and alcohol abuse

        (5) Delinquency and vandalism

    c. American Medical Association White Paper on Adolescent Health (1987)

2. Classroom related changes

    a. Improve self-concept (which has been demonstrated to improve academic performance)

    b. Improve classroom behavior

    c. Improve self-responsibility and good citizenship

    d. Improve social skills

3. Attending group is more acceptable than going to counseling—individual or at an outside agency

    a. School setting more acceptable place to receive help than mental health clinic and/or private practitioner's office

        (1) Students become comfortable more readily

        (2) More familiar with person and setting

        (3) Better coordination

    b. Less threatening than individual counseling due to diffuse focus

4. Provides an opportunity to identify and further evaluate students who might need more intensive intervention

5. Assists the staff by improving professional skills

C. EXPANSION OF COUNSELING PROGRAM

1. Better use of Counselor time

   a. Greater numbers in more depth

   b. Consistent with learning outcomes for developmental guidance program of study

2. Meets perceived needs of staff and students

   a. Students must cope with stress of growing up

   b. Students have obstacles to learning

   c. Schools must deal with life issues that confront students, e.g., divorce, death, drug abuse

   d. Schools must deal with discipline problems

3. Primary prevention program, e.g., drugs, alcohol, suicide, runaway, drop-out, pregnancy, delinquency, vandalism

D. BENEFIT FOR STUDENTS

1. Provides place to share cognitive and affective material not appropriately aired in the classroom

    a. Increases ability to communicate feelings and ideas

    b. Teaches appropriate feedback techniques

    c. Teaches universality—"you are not alone"

    d. Instills hope, motivation and direction

2. Provides opportunity for self-examination

    a. Teaches students to trust, disclose, ask for help, be assertive, and address the needs of others

    b. Enhances self-esteem

    c. Teaches students good citizenship and responsibility for their own behavior

    d. Improves interpersonal and social skills

    e. Provides valuable milieu for non-verbal students

3. Assists in mastery of age-related developmental tasks

    a. Attainment of separation

    b. Development of a personal moral value system

    c. Commitment to career choice

    d. Capacity to be intimate

    e. Establishment of sexual identity

4. For Troubled Students

    a. Provides objective listener with expertise

    b. Provides outlet for trapped feelings

    c. Offers support and understanding

    d. Provides insight into problem behavior

    e. Impedes recurrence of initial problems

THERAPEUTIC IMPACT ON
THE SCHOOL MILIEU

A. GROUP AS A SUBSYSTEM OF THE SCHOOL

1. Systems theory approach

    a. Not an extension of individual counseling

    b. Reflects dynamics of entire school

    c. Leader can learn and share dynamics of school with other faculty and staff (after termination of project year)

B. CONTINUOUS INTERPLAY BETWEEN SCHOOL AND COUNSELING GROUP

1. Encourages the sharing of information in group that is not generally shared in the classroom

2. Key variable is the degree of contact when not in group

    a. Provides knowledge of each other beyond group involvement itself

    b. Adolescent enters group with different data base

        (1) Problems

        (2) Daily experiences

3. Determinants of adolescent behavior in the group

    a. Personal dynamics

    b. Influence of school setting

4. Group functions more like inpatient (hospital) group than out-patient (office group)

    a. Contact outside group

    b. Increased data base

5. Different patterns of interaction among and between group members and group leader

C. EFFECTIVENESS OF GROUP PROCESS IS INTENSIFIED

1. Knowledge from within and outside group is shared

2. Feedback

   a. More direct

   b. Honest

   c. Undeniable

   d. Observed

3. Group recapitulates primary family problems

   a. Learn to deal with "authority figures"

      (1) Leader and secondary leader become like father and mother

   b. Sibling rivalry

      (1) Group members become like brothers and sisters

4. Separation-individuation issues

5. Need to reduce friction of "living together"

   a. Provides a vehicle for working through problem behaviors such as

      (1) "Tattle tale"

      (2) "Impress the leader"

      (3) "Wait 'til group"

      (4) "Show-off"

6. Can usually control attendance

   a. Group is treated as a class

D. ISSUES TO ADDRESS IN SCHOOL COUNSELING GROUPS

1. Fear that disclosed material might be shared outside the group (in school)

    a. Anxiety provoking

    b. Excessive sensitivity

    c. Ambivalence about sharing

    d. Guilt

2. May not be able to control who is included

    a. May have students who are not motivated

    b. In the first year, try to "stack the deck" with good members

    c. All participants must agree to be in the group

3. Teacher expectations too high

BASIC ELEMENTS IN GROUP LEADERSHIP

A. PERSONAL ATTRIBUTES AND SKILLS OF THE LEADER

1. Positive self-concept and strong sense of self-awareness

2. Positive feeling toward adolescents

3. Already trusted and sought out by students on informal basis

4. Feel positive about ability to handle the group

   a. Normal to be apprehensive about:

      (1) Is group constructed properly?

      (2) What will dynamics of group be?

      (3) Will leader and secondary leader function well together?

5. Good role model able to teach (through example) principles of psychologically healthy functioning

   a. Openness and honesty

   b. Acceptance

   c. Congruence

   d. Genuineness

   e. Unconditional positive regard

6. Model group behavior—act in the way you want group members to act

   a. Accurate feedback

b. Don't monopolize

c. Talk about feelings

7. Interact with each member

a. Every group member will speak, even if only in the summary

b. Make good eye contact with each group member

8. Promote member-to-member interaction

a. Their group, not yours

b. Do not take group silence personally

c. Talk to each other, not to the leaders

9. Know sociology of the group

a. The group atmosphere

b. Group alliances

(1) Seating arrangement

(2) Who talks to whom

10. Not necessary to have dynamic understanding of psychopathology

a. Know normal vs. abnormal

b. Know when to seek help

11. Technical expert

a. Know essential principles of group dynamics

b. Know essential principles of group leadership

c. Know when to take group member for additional help

12. Leader is the only one who knows what a good group is

B. LEADER MUST UNDERSTAND TRANSFERENCE AND COUNTER-TRANSFERENCE

1. Transference—the feelings that the members of the group have for and about the group leader

   a. May reflect feelings for significant others

   b. Transfer these feelings to group members

2. Countertransference—the feelings that the leader develops toward all or certain group members

   a. May reflect personal issues

   b. Normal, but non-productive if not recognized and dealt with

C. LEADERS AND MEMBERS MUST DEVELOP REALISTIC EXPECTATIONS FOR THE GROUP

1. Clear understanding of what can and what cannot be accomplished in the group setting

   a. Leader

   b. Member

   c. Parent

   d. School administration

      (1) Must accept that they cannot know specifics of what occurs in the group

   e. School board

      (1) Must accept that they cannot know specifics of what occurs in the group

2. Level of intensity

   a. Feelings

   b. Content

3. "The ego of the group is always greater than the sum of its parts" [Marrone, Thomas. (1977). *The Project at Number Twenty Three,* Norristown, PA.]

   a. The group will not let the leader go too indepth too soon or too fast

   b. The group members will act-up in some way to accomplish this

D. PURPOSE OF THE GROUP

1. All group activities should relate to the goals of the group

    a. Issues of adolescent passage

    b. Talking about feelings

2. All group activities should be directed to assist the adolescent in mastery of the developmental tasks

3. Group as a "transitional object"

E. MUST AGREE TO THE GOALS OF GROUP COUNSELING

1. To improve self-concept

2. To increase self-responsibility

3. To improve adolescent's interactional patterns

4. To provide support, inspiration, improve social skills and insight into problem behaviors

5. Result will be both symptom relief and personality change

F. HOW WILL THIS AGREEMENT BE REACHED?

1. Contract

    a. Signed agreement

    b. Mutual understanding

    c. Verbal commitment

2. Contract is really an understanding

    a. Not a legal document

    b. Not a promise

        (1) Instills guilt

3. Clear Expectations

4. Individual Interview

5. Reaffirmed in the group process itself

NOTES

STRUCTURING THE ADOLESCENT COUNSELING GROUP

A. STRUCTURE—EXTENT TO WHICH GROUP MEMBERS ARE CLEAR ABOUT WHAT BEHAVIORS ARE EXPECTED OF THEM

1. What leader will do

2. What members will do

3. What will take place within the group setting

B. MOST IMPORTANT AND PRIMARY FUNCTION OF THE GROUP LEADER

1. "Lack of structure is the single most important reason for failure of a group"

2. Evidence of lack of structure

   a. Increased anxiety

   b. Fear is evident

   c. Expectations become unrealistic

   d. Behavior of students

      (1) Acting out

      (2) Joking

      (3) Fidgety

   e. Leader talks more frequently

3. Once structure is in place, content will be supplied by group members.

   a. Reason for no curriculum or planned activities

A **MEMBERS HOW TO OPERATE** *THEIR*

ιe members', not the leader's

ιnd boundaries

ιe of comfort and security

ιembers from physical or emotional harm

εcide what the group will discuss

D. BASIS OF THE STRUCTURE

1. Rules and expectations

2. Goals and purposes

3. Consistency of implementing the group program

    a. Setting

    b. Record keeping

    c. Methodology

4. RAPP

    a. Rules

    b. Approach

    c. Purpose

    d. Phases

E. BASIC PREMISE OF *ADOLESCENT GROUP COUNSELING IN SCHOOLS PROJECT*

1. No topics or planned activities for each group

   a. Implication if topics or activities are used

      (1) Gives common statements and experiences to start

      (2) Leader in control

      (3) Increases dependency

      (4) Creates "game of the week" atmosphere

   b. Research (Leiberman, Yalom, & Mites, 1973)

      (1) Large numbers of activities

         (a) Popular with the group

         (b) Lower outcome level

      (2) Bypasses early stages of group

      (3) Group remains superficial

      (4) Accentuates leader centered group

      (5) Decreases group effectiveness

         (a) Better for short-term groups than long-term groups

2. No curriculum; the structure provided by the leader is sufficient

3. "When the mind is ready, a teacher appears."

4. Want group members to take responsibility for the group

5. Want the members to focus on processing of thoughts and feelings

NOTES

V

TASKS OF GROUP LEADERSHIP—OVERVIEW
(In order of importance)

A. CONSTRUCT THE GROUP

B. MAINTAIN CONTROL AND PROVIDE PROTECTION

C. FACILITATE PROCESSING OF THOUGHTS AND FEELINGS

D. PROVIDE INSIGHT INTO PROBLEM BEHAVIOR

1. Least important function

2. More significant if provided by the members

3. Will only happen if other three tasks are performed satisfactorily

NOTES

CONSTRUCTING THE GROUP—TASK ONE

A. GROUP COMPOSITION—PRIMARY AND SECONDARY LEADER

1. Primary Leader

   a. Overall responsibility

   b. More verbal and active than secondary leader

   c. Individual interviews

   d. Writes summary

   e. Group observation checklist (See Sample 19 in Sample Materials Section of this book)

2. Secondary Leader

   a. Support person

   b. Monitor the process

   c. Collects and disposes of group summaries

   d. Group observation checklist (See Sample 19 in Sample Materials Section of this book)

   e. Less verbal

   f. Broaden the area of interaction

      (1) Frequently can be used to break a one-to-one interaction between leader and member

      (2) Shift focus from one person to another

         (a) Verbally
         (b) Subtle non-verbal clues

   g. Increases opportunities for identification with significant others

   h. Provides good role model

i. Adds relevant and pertinent information when appropriate

j. Picks up slack

k. Most importantly—cues the primary leader as to dynamics and events that may be occurring in the group

l. Provides feedback to primary leader after group

   (1) Transference/countertransference

   (2) Keeping primary leader honest

m. Meet—before and after each group session

   (1) 7 P's (Proper prior planning prevents pitifully poor performance)

   (2) Planning ongoing process

   (3) Process events of the group

   (4) Review group-plan strategy for next group

n. Be scrupulously careful of where and when you discuss the group

   (1) Do not discuss a just completed session as you walk down the hall with your secondary leader—members are everywhere, and are listening

   (2) Members are extremely observant of what the leaders are doing and concerned about confidentiality

   (3) Other faculty are very interested in group but should not be allowed to know what takes place within the group

o. If a particular group's primary or secondary leader is absent on the day their group meets

   (1) Group can carry on with only one group leader

   (2) Do not have anyone "fill in" for the absent leader

   (3) Give a brief explanation as to where the other leader is and proceed as usual

   (4) If you know in advance that you will not be in group the next week, inform the group personally

p. It is important that primary leader stay in the group while secondary leader insures full group attendance

   (1) If child leaves group, secondary leader goes after the child and resolves situation

   (2) If child is late for group, primary leader stays secondary leader goes and gets that member

(a) Early in the year members may forget, may be too scared and/or may not want to come to group

(b) Later not a problem

[1] Unless form of resistance

3. Choice of primary and secondary leader based on

   a. "Goodness of fit"

   b. Staff availability

   c. Type of group

   d. Leadership style

   e. Personality of the group leaders

   f. Composition of the group itself

4. Secondary leader becomes primary leader the following year

   a. One year's experience without pressure of being primary leader

5. Secondary leader gets more active and verbal as the group progresses through the developmental stage

   a. Secondary leader must help get group started in the distrust stages.

   b. Be less active in the intergration stage

   c. Reactivate in the working stage

   d. "E.F. Hutton" of the group

6. Dynamics between primary and secondary leader are key and complex

   a. Role of primary and secondary must be separate and distinct

   b. Must be clear to group members

     (1) Initial interviews

     (2) Opening and closing questions

       (a) "What do you want to talk about today?"

       (b) "How did group go today and how did you do?"

c. Leader makes it happen but frequently it is the secondary leader who can really tell what actually occurred in the group

d. Secondary leader must position at level between power position of primary leader and level of group members

   (1) Perceived as less powerful

   (2) Can confront and elicit behavior in a less threatening manner

       (a) Especially important in the working stage

           [1] Move member "off dead center"

           [2] Manipulate change in the group

           [3] Intervene when necessary

e. Avoid rivalry at all cost

   (1) Avoid conflict

   (2) Avoid splitting

       (a) Good and bad each in a separate place

       (b) "Good guy"—"bad guy"

       (c) Cognitive dissonance

       (d) Members play "Mommy off Daddy"

           [1] "I've got a secret"

           [2] "I'm really important to him"

f. Like good marriage

   (1) Communication is essential

   (2) Openness and honesty

   (3) High level of respect and trust

g. Not alike but complimentary

h. Way primary and secondary leader interact provides good role model

   (1) How to relate

   (2) How to handle differences

i. Does not make significant difference if leaders are the same sex or opposite sex except in early adolescence

(1) Early adolescent—opposite sex is better because of identification issues

(2) Either same sex or opposite sex recapitulates primary family

    (a) Fantasy: primary and secondary leaders are romantically involved

    (b) Expected, yes—defended, not necessarily

        [1] Only if directly addressed by group members

(3) Helpful for role modeling

    (a) Transference

    (b) Can confront splitting of mother and father at home

    (c) Microcosm of the macrocosm

7. Within group setting, primary and secondary leader sit directly opposite each other

   a. Supervisory camera focused on primary leader

   b. Secondary leader sits with camera at back

8. Primary and secondary leader enter group together

   a. Put tape in camera

   b. Start camera

   c. Go to assigned seats

   d. Allow group members to finish reading notes

   e. Notes are passed to secondary leader

   f. Secondary leader destroys notes in front of group members

   g. Places destroyed notes in envelope

   h. Primary leader takes care of any business matters; then asks

   i. "What do you want to talk about today?"

B. MAKE-UP OF THE GROUP MEMBERS

1. Proper balance and blending essential

2. Eight to ten students

   a. Ten members is best

      (1) Greater pool to draw upon

      (2) A student may transfer out of school

   b. More than ten too difficult to manage

   c. Four least possible number of members to conduct a group

      (1) Small groups far more leader dependent

         (a) Group leaders must be more verbal

      (2) Issue is survival

      (3) Leader should question members regarding issue of survival

3. Equal numbers of boys and girls

   a. Unless single sex group

4. First year choose students with realistic potential for change

   a. Build track record within building, among staff, administration, etc.

   b. Must tackle some of the school's problem adolescents to establish credibility

5. Three general types of students needed for program

   a. "Model students" do not appear to have significant problems or issues

      (1) Provide good role models

      (2) Make group participation more acceptable among the rest of the student body

      (3) Faces issues of "growing-up" just like any other adolescent

      (4) Frequently, model students have problems also

         (a) Trying to be "perfect"

         (b) Peer relations

(c) "Responsible hero"

b. "Problem students" behavior problems, acting-out type of student

    (1) Most commonly referred

    (2) Do not take too many, despite pressure to do so

c. "Issue students"—problem in the family, death, injury, divorce, withdrawn, academic problems

    (1) Do not act out but have "things on their mind"

    (2) Benefit from knowing "they are not alone"

6. The mix of the group is the key to success

a. Two discipline problems

b. Two model students

c. One withdrawn child

d. Remaining three to five from

    (1) Discipline problems

    (2) Academic problems

    (3) Social issue e.g. suicide, drug usage, sexual promiscuity

    (4) Emotional difficulties

e. Must have at least three to four highly verbal members

    (1) Some of these will be identified problem students but must be verbal as well

    (2) Most verbal group member should be a model and/or a positive influence

f. Under achievers as well as good academic students

g. Adolescents with good social skills as well as those who are not very socially skilled

7. Choice of exclusion

a. "Bad" choice can be destructive

b. Avoid too many of any one type of problem (diagnosis)

c. Avoid too many behavior disordered students

(1) Power battles

(2) Subgrouping

d. Avoid florid psychotics

(1) Can gain too much sympathy

(2) Can be too disruptive and too time consuming

8. Homogeneous vs. heterogeneous groups

a. Homogeneous for ego strength, life experiences, etc.

(1) "It is the similarities that bring people together but it is their differences that help them grow"

b. Heterogeneous for problems

c. Avoid homogeneous grouping for specific problems in which behavior is involved such as

(1) Socially and emotionally disturbed

(2) Learning disabled

(3) Drop-out potential

d. It can be satisfactory to homogeneous group for some categories such as

(1) Gifted

(2) Diabetic

(3) Sexually abused

(4) Pregnancy

9. Eventually, all groups become heterogeneous

a. Specialized knowledge needed by leader for initial sessions

b. Process, goals, tasks, and techniques remain essentially the same throughout

c. After the unique characteristic of the group is dealt with, the focus shifts to heterogeneous issues

d. However, it takes longer for homogeneous groups to become cohesive and to progress through the developmental stages of groups

10. Age and grade groupings

a. Place children based on chronological age rather than grade

b. Place children based on developmental age rather than calendar age

c. No more than two years apart

    (1) Important not to have adolescents with vast differences in worldliness and experiences

d. Place 5th and 6th grade students separately

e. If 7th grade is first year in a new school, place them separately

f. If 7th grade is not, then 7th and 8th grade may be placed together

g. If 9th grade is first year in a new school, place them separately

h. If 9th grade is not, then 9th and 10th grade may be placed together

i. Seniors (12th grade) should be placed separately

    (1) Issues of graduation and leaving

    (2) "King of hill" and not wanting to appear to be vulnerable

C. INDIVIDUAL INTERVIEWS

1. Prior to admission to the program each child is given an individual interview

   a. Conducted by group leader (secondary leader can be present)

   b. Consideration should be given to

      (1) Time involved

      (2) Two adults and one child might be overpowering

   c. If time is limited primary and secondary leader can split group into two

      (1) Primary leader takes members from whom it might be more difficult to obtain consent

      (2) Secondary leader takes model and/or easier students

      (3) Also consider who has greater contact and alliance with certain students

2. Purpose

   a. Screen for suitability

   b. Obtain data base regarding nature of difficulties

   c. Determine problem solving abilities

   d. Assess motivation

   e. Develop therapeutic alliance

   f. Work through resistance

   g. Goal is to "seduce" member into participation

   h. Obtain verbal commitment to participate

   i. Obtain agreement to abide by the rules

3. Individual Interview must

   a. Explain purpose and rationale

   b. Explain selection process

      (1) How many students

      (2) Why

        (a) Do not tell potential group member reason for their selection

           [1] If problem, they already know

        (b) State purpose of group (see RAPP)

      (3) Identify leader and secondary leader

  c. Where and when group will meet

    (1) Location

    (2) Describe setting

    (3) If problems with teacher notify group leader

  d. Explain video-taping

    (1) Supervision

    (2) Emphasize who will be allowed to see tapes and who will not

    (3) Stress confidentiality

  e. Obtain agreement to participate

  f. Obtain agreement to abide by rules

4. See Script of Individual Interview (See Sample 11 in Sample Materials Section of this book)

5. Leader must communicate

  a. Group's purpose

  b. Nature of group process

  c. Behaviors and activities that members will be expected to perform (i.e., rules of group)

  d. Potential risks of participating

  e. Voluntary nature of participating

    (1) Member has to say "yes" to be admitted

    (2) Member has to agree to abide by the rules of group

6. Offer information and instructions about goals, expectations, and hopes for group

  a. Teach how group operates

  b. See Sample 10, Office Letter of Invitation for Group Participation, in the Sample Materials Section of this book.

7. Determine if the member has some problems or issues they might like to work on in the group

   a. Try to obtain commitment to work actively on that problem or issue

8. Listen carefully to their reaction

   a. Metaphors and Images

   b. Through the use of these, potential group members will reveal their own personal fears, objections, etc.

9. Written contract is questionable but a minimum therapeutic contract is necessary

   a. Clear expectations of function, roles, and behaviors

   b. Commitment to abide by the rules of group

   c. Rules

      (1) What's said in group, stays in group

      (2) One person talks at a time

      (3) No one leaves without permission

   d. Visitor rules

      (1) Must obtain permission to attend from the group

      (2) Rules

         (a) Must identify themselves and why they are observing

         (b) May not participate

         (c) Must share feedback with the group at the end of group

   e. Do not make rules you cannot enforce

      (1) Subgrouping

         (a) Will occur within the group

      (2) Outside group contact

         (a) Has to occur in a school group

         (b) Provides "grist for the mill"

         (c) Do not allow "I've got a secret", have group members share outside material in the group

         (d) Avoid "search and siege" game

         (e) Do not allow sharing of information about students not present in the group

D. PARENT MEETING

1. Group meeting prior to first session

    a. See letter of invitation and consent form (See Sample 2, Letter of Invitation to Parents—First Year, and Sample 3, Consent Form Sent to Parents, in Sample Materials Section of this Book)

    b. Agenda

        (1) Overview of adolescent issues

        (2) Overview of group counseling program

        (3) Question and answer session

    c. Purpose of meeting to clarify

        (1) Goals

        (2) Expectations

        (3) Procedures

            (a) Explain completion of Burks Behavior Rating Scale by parent

        (4) Parents informed of possible manipulations to expect

            (a) Anxiety provoking nature of group

            (b) "Stories" told by children who wish to drop out

        (5) Parent support essential component

    d. Goal

        (1) Obtain parent support

        (2) Obtain written consent

2. Individual meeting with parents only if necessary

    a. Consider telephone call if needed

3. May want to consider

    a. Collateral parents' group

    b. "Parent Night" program (See Sample 9, Letter of Invitation to Parents—First Year, in Sample Materials Section of this book)

E. PHYSICAL SETTING

1. Essential to the structure of the group is the consistency of the setting

   a. Location

   b. Furniture

   c. Same day—"Sacred Tuesdays"

      (1) Group not cancelled

      (2) No tests scheduled

      (3) No field trips, assemblies, etc.

      (4) Best if groups are not done on Mondays or Fridays

   d. Same time

2. Minimize interruptions and disruptions

   a. Unavoidable

      (1) Fire drills

      (2) Messages over intercom

   b. Just part of "normal" day

   c. Ignore as much as possible

3. All group sessions meet once per week for one class period

4. Group begins at the end of September or early October

   a. Must be early enough to insure at least 30 sessions

5. Seating arrangement

   a. Chairs in a circle with nothing in front

      (1) No desk

      (2) No materials (pencil, paper, books) to hold on to

      (3) Summary placed on chairs of group members

      (4) No assigned seats-allow students to choose

(5) If a member is absent, leave chair in the circle

(6) If member leaves group permanently, remove the chair

   b. Leaders sit opposite each other-in same seats all year

   c. Camera positioned to focus on primary leader

6. Sign on door—"Group in Session"

7. Clock in room

8. Daily bulletin should list the periods group is being held to insure staff awareness

9. Attendance

   a. Groups are fixed entities (as much as possible)

      (1) Do not change leaders

      (2) Do not change members (with rare exceptions)

   b. Regular attendance is key

   c. Members are made aware; the more continuous the group, the better

F. ADDITION AND TERMINATION OF GROUP MEMBERS

1. Adding members

   a. ***Adolescent Group Counseling in School's Project***—group members are never added after the second week of the program

   b. Timing crucial

      (1) Not when group is in crisis

      (2) Not when group is in a new phase

   c. Old group members say they want new members, but they really may not

      (1) Rite of initiation

         (a) Hostility

         (b) "Good old days"

         (c) "Reminds me of John"

   d. Good to add in pairs but not more than two at a time

      (1) Partner for security (ally)

      (2) Less threatening to each of them and to the group

      (3) Less disruptive to the group than one at a time

   e. Prepare both old and new members

      (1) Share members' first group experiences

      (2) "You all remember how you felt"

      (3) During initial interview

         (a) Forewarn new members of possible group reaction

         (b) Rite of initiation

      (4) Have group members state rules of group

         (a) Secure agreement

         (b) Place statement of agreement in next week's summary

   f. Most important—addition of a new member causes the group to regress

2. Dropouts

   a. Must process with the group due to group cohesiveness

b. Essential that the student "take the chair" after the distrust stage

c. Must process feelings about the situation

    (1) Feelings about the situation

        (a) Anger

        (b) Guilt

        (c) Fear

    (2) Feelings about change

    (3) Process to follow after member leaves

    (4) Confidentiality

d. Once member leaves, that person cannot be discussed

    (1) Members will fear that if they leave or miss group they will be talked about

3. Termination of the unsuccessful group member at leader's discretion

a. Very rarely done

b. Not recommended without consultation

c. If you do, see individually

    (1) Process the situation

    (2) Take responsibility to secure help in another setting

d. Process with group

    (1) Anger at member

    (2) Anger at leader

    (3) Concern for break of confidentiality

e. Terminating someone from the group threatens the group

f. Usually no matter how disruptive, group will support that person

    (1) "There, but for the grace of God, go I"

    (2) Blame will focus on the group leader

4. Termination of the successful group member

a. Stronger bonding to healthier member' therefore, termination is not easy

(1) "Taking the chair"

    (a) Indicate progress made

    (b) Serves as motivator for remaining group members

b. "Graduation exercise"

    (1) Feelings mixed—glad and sad

    (2) Remind members it is a goal that has been achieved

c. Group member may not want to leave

    (1) May choose to regress and/or misbehave

    (2) Reason

        (a) To show not ready to leave

        (b) To elicit angry response from leader or group members to make it easier to leave

    (3) Parable of the "Chicken and the Eagle" [James, M., & Jongeward, D. (1971). **Born to Win.** Addison Wesley/Signet, pp. 105-106.]

d. Reasons students drop out of group [Yalom, I.D. (1985). **Theory and Practice of Group Psychotherapy,** pp. 231-243. New York: Basic Books.]

    (1) External factors

        (a) Leave school

        (b) Change in schedule

    (2) Group defiance

    (3) Inadequate orientation for counseling

    (4) Complications from subgrouping

        (a) Dating-breakup in relationship

        (b) Broken promise

    (5) Problems of intimacy

        (a) Self-disclosure too much, too early

    (6) Fear of emotional contagion

        (a) Want to be involved

            [1] Scared

[2] Do not know how

(7) Inability to share counselor

(8) Early confrontation

(9) Competition between individual and group counseling

e. Major reason for drop-out: inadequate preparation for group initially

f. Dropouts

(1) Do not let the dropout threaten the leader

(2) Do not let the dropout threaten the group

(3) Must be identified as the dropout's problem and as a form of resistance

(4) Remind group members of the contract for participation

(5) To facilitate support of the group and reduce hositility

(a) Suggest dropout might do better the second time around, or in another group

(b) If appropriate, indicate how the dropout did not complete his contract

5. Termination for the Summer (school groups)

a. Remind students of progress made

b. Encourage use of new strengths

c. Share telephone numbers

(1) Not in the group

(2) Encourage members to call each other

d. Encourage summer activity program involvement

6. Termination Activities will be discussed in later section on page 146 and in Supervision Session #7.

G. RECORD KEEPING

1. Post-group discussion should result in some written documentation of the session

    a. Legal purposes

    b. For review and planning

2. Primary and secondary leader prepare a summary of previous session to be shared with group

    a. One copy kept for record and never brought to the group

        (1) Keep in coordinator's office

    b. Other copies placed on chairs prior to each group

    c. Copies destroyed during group in presence of everyone

3. Summary written in note form

    a. Includes each person's name

    b. *Or* general summary

    c. See Sample 14, Group Notes, Name by Name Format and Sample 15, Group Notes, Summary Format, in Sample Materials Section of this book

4. If group members are unable to read summary, primary leader reads it at beginning of the group

    a. If only one or two cannot read, it is possible to read it to them sometime during day, before group

5. Group notes serve greater purpose than "just" to summarize last week's group

6. Purpose of group summary

    a. Document events of group

    b. Bridges "time" between each group session

        (1) Improves memory of events

        (2) Valuable if someone was absent

        (3) Helps group move into the "here and now" more easily

    c. Can manipulate the discussion

7. Content

    a. What was discussed and shared

    b. Remind members of major issues addressed *or* not addressed

    c. To lead the discussion for next session (plant seeds)

    d. Reinforce positive experience

    e. Discourage inappropriate behavior

    f. Create a focus without leader having to verbalize that focus

8. Note—group leader should never take notes within the group or during the group session

NOTES

CONDUCTING THE FIRST GROUP

A. FIRST GROUP SESSION IS VITAL

1. Leaders are the most active they will ever be

    a. Define procedures and rules

        (1) Explain Scheduling

        (2) Make-up classes

        (3) Tell them they may contact you if they run into classroom problems (scheduling, make-up work, etc.)

    b. Establish rationale for group

        (1) Kids listen to kids before adults

        (2) Safe place to air problems

        (3) Many alternative solutions to problems presented

    c. Give expectations

    d. Teach them what group is about

        (1) Tell them what you're going to tell them

        (2) Tell them

        (3) Tell them what you told them

    e. Stress importance of group experience

        (1) Positive experience

        (2) Help them grow as people

        (3) Develop adult skills

    f. Predict possible problems

g. Help them understand how they relate to each other

    (1) Opportunity to share positive feedback

    (2) Will feel less isolated and alone

    (3) Help each other; support system

    (4) Learn own strengths and weaknesses

    (5) Become more comfortable with each other

    (6) Gain confidence in self

h. "Set the stage"

2. Leader

    a. Fearful—anxious

        (1) Students feel similar

        (2) Share these feelings with them

        (3) "Stranger" anxiety

    b. Knows importance of the first meeting

    c. Fears loss of intimacy with individual students

    d. Fear of self-disclosing inappropriately

    e. The only one who knows what a "good" group is really like

3. Group member

    a. Appropriately anxious

        (1) Threatening situation; totally new experience

        (2) Desires to make a good impression on leader and other group members

        (3) Lacks clear-cut conceptualization of what to expect

            (a) Personal role

            (b) Role of others

            (c) Role of leader

       [1] Perceive you as a teacher

       [2] Question change in your role

b. Distrustful; suspicious

c. Fearful of losing control

d. May or may not be angry about being in group

e. Fear of doing or saying the wrong thing

f. Does not know how to become part of group (belonging) and also remain an individual

     (1) Major issue of the adolescent passage

B. DYAD TECHNIQUE (First Group Session)

1. Ice breaker—anxiety reducer

    a. Pair members off, each member interviews the other

       (1) Group of ten will break into five pairs of two

       (2) 3 to 5 minutes to gather information (10 minutes total)

       (3) Pair as follows

           (a) Leaders introduce each other

           (b) If nine members, secondary leader pairs with a student and primary leader introduces him or herself

    b. Stated goal: to introduce the person they interview

       (1) Urge them to be extensive in gathering information

       (2) Interviewer will be introduced by interviewee

2. Also used to demonstrate

    a. Easier to discuss facts than feelings

    b. Most Dyad information is factual

       (1) Not anxiety they feel about group

       (2) Not apprehension they feel about group

    c. Generates discussion

       (1) Guide them into how hard it is to discuss own feelings

       (2) Keep it going as long as it runs well

       (3) Total time about ½ class period

    d. May take entire class period

       (1) Okay if you do not get to RAPP

       (2) Do it next time

C. VIDEO TAPE AND CAMERA

1. Important learning tool

    a. Present it matter-of-factly

    b. Use it to monitor leaders in supervision

    c. Primary and secondary leader use it to monitor themselves

2. Camera aimed at leader

3. Tapes viewed by supervisor, and group leaders *only*

    a. Assure them that parents, friends, principal, etc. *will never* view the tapes

    b. After every four sessions, all tapes are erased and taped over again

4. Video tape and camera will not be issue if you do not make them one

    a. Let them turn around and look at the camera

    b. Perhaps wave to "supervisor"

    c. Then ignore it

D. RAPP—RULES, APPROACH, PURPOSE, AND PHASES (Second Group Session)

1. Purpose of RAPP

   a. Teach members how to operate their group

   b. Gives boundaries and landmarks to hold onto for security

   c. To interpret deviations from it

2. Rules—(review of initial interview)

   a. Stated and rationale given

      (1) Confidentiality

         (a) Most important rule

         (b) "What's said in group, stays in group"

         (c) Builds trust in each other

         (d) Promotes honesty in discussions

         (e) Members may tell own parents what they said, but not what anyone else said

         (f) Leaders are bound by same restrictions, with one exception (see g. that follows):

         (g) Leader lives by school rules

            [1] Must report suicidal, sexual or physical abuse

            [2] Will not violate confidence on any issue

               [a] Would not have spoken up in group if the member did not want to deal with it

               [b] Take the group member to counselor with you to report incident

               [c] Result is sign of support and caring rather than break of confidentiality

            [3] No foul language or cursing

               [a] Not productive or necessary

         (h) Don't discuss anyone absent from group that day

      (2) One person talks at a time

         (a) Too many talking—no one listens

         (b) Might miss something of importance

(c) You learn when you listen, not when you talk

(d) Everyone benefits from others' ideas

    [1] Listening is also working

    [2] May be able to add or clarify

(3) No one leaves room without permission

(a) With only one session per week, much time can be lost

(b) Anger may prompt escape

    [1] Need to stay and learn from it

    [2] Purpose of group

    [3] "Can't run away from your problems, because they always travel with you"

    [4] Develops skills of learning to give and receive feedback

b. Contract establishment

(1) "Do we all have the rules and understand?"

(2) "Can we all live with these rules?"

(a) Obtain verbal affirmation

(b) Everyone in the group verbal or with head nod must agree in front of everyone else to abide by the rules of group

(c) Comment, "Anyone not okay with them?"

c. Rules restated whenever new member is added

d. Explanation of summary sheet

(1) "Minutes" of previous session

(2) Will be waiting on seats at start of each group

(a) Read silently by members

(b) May be read aloud by leader if necessary-leader option

(3) Sheets do not leave room

(a) Destroyed—in front of members by secondary leader, before opening statement

(b) Done routinely, the flow of the session is not broken

3. Approach

    a. "Here and Now" [Yalom, L. (1985). ***The Theory and Practice of Group Psychotherapy.*** New York: Basic Books.]

        (1) Based on interpersonal theory

            (a) Problems in relating to other people

            (b) Group reflects what happens outside the group

        (2) Member does not have to tell the leader personal problems

            (a) Observed in group

            (b) Group microcosm of the macrocosm

        (3) Leader creates the environment to activate the processing of feelings and teaches the group members how to examine their feelings

        (4) Self-reflecting loop—Process the Process (Figure 1)

            (a) Event takes place (x)

            (b) Process the event (y)

            (c) Data gathered is for group to work on (z)

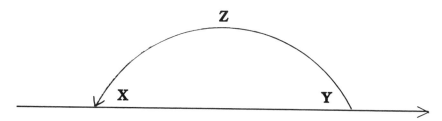

Figure 1. Self-reflecting loop.

        (5) Process is necessary but not sufficient; must relate the group behavior to the adolescent's individual problems outside the group

        (6) How the member processes, reacts to and deals with feelings is the key variable

            (a) Members must examine their own feelings

            (b) Members must learn to accept responsibility for their feelings and not blame others

            (c) How you react is the key variable

            (d) "Wave" story

                Two boys are on a beach. A wave comes along and knocks the two boys down. One gets up, laughs and stands up to wait for the next wave. The other one gets up and runs to his mother yelling "Mommy, Mommy, the wave knocked me down." It was the same wave; why was the wave fun for one boy and scary for the other? Clearly, it was the reaction the boys had to the wave that made the difference.

    (e) A total stranger passes you by in the street and says, "You look awful." You keep walking and ignore the comment. Your best friend sees you in the hall in school and says "You look awful." You go to the bathroom and look in the mirror to check it out. Why?

    (f) You tell a person how you feel about what they say or do; how that person reacts to what you tell them is their responsibility.

(7) The "here and now" approach is designed to focus the group on

    (a) Relationships

        [1] Learning to get along better

    (b) Communication patterns

    (c) Immediate feelings of members

        [1] Not current events from outside life

        [2] Not past events

        [3] "Don't tell me what you think—tell me how you feel"

(8) Leader must set the example to activate "here and now" feelings, e.g.,

    (a) Express own nervousness

    (b) "Does anyone else feel that way?"

4. Purpose

   a. Improve self-concept

      (1) How a person feels about himself

      (2) Greatest predictor of success

   b. Improve ability to accept responsibility for our own behavior

      (1) Give examples

         (a) Being on time

         (b) Doing things correctly

         (c) Getting homework in

         (d) Being dependable

      (2) Accept consequences for our own behavior

         (a) "Blame game" (she made me do it)

         (b) "When you point the finger, three come back"

   c. Improve ability to get along with people

      (1) Interpersonal relations

         (a) Peers

         (b) Teachers

         (c) Parents

      (2) Say what you mean and mean what you say

         (a) A friend tells you what you **need** to hear—not what you **want** to hear

         (b) Our behavior affects others

5. Phases

   a. Four stages of development all groups go through

      (1) **Distrust stage** (Sessions 1-6)

         (a) Sizing each other up

         (b) Wonder how you fit in group

         (c) Apprehensive and scared

         (d) Similarity to making a new friendship—When you first meet somebody you don't tell them your deepest, darkest secrets; rather what you do is tell them a little bit about yourself to see if they can be trusted. The better you get to know them and find out that they can be trusted and do care about you, the more you share. That is what group is like; a series of friendships with a group of people. With time, you will learn to trust and to share

      (2) **Integration Stage** (Sessions 6-15)

         (a) Become more comfortable with being in group

         (b) Become closer and more honest

         (c) Learn how to keep to group topics

         (d) Discuss things in common

         (e) Leader will begin to be less involved in discussions

      (3) **Working Stage** (Sessions 15-27)

         (a) Here and now

            [1] Will learn what is an appropriate group topic

            [2] Will stay "on-task" more

         (b) Work on significant issues

            [1] Will freely discuss relevant issues

            [2] Will share true feelings, without fear of looking or sounding foolish

         (c) Trust apparent

            [1] Will share things not appropriately shared anywhere else

            [2] Will receive information from others with compassion and understanding

         (d) Desire to help each other

             [1] Truly care about the members of the group

             [2] Enter into a "family-type" relationship

        (4) **Termination** (Sessions 27-30)

            (a) End of group for the school year

            (b) "Taking the chair"

            (c) Special ending for group taught during Supervision #7

    b. Each individual group session recapitulates the phases that occur in the lifetime of the group

        (1) Each individual session will go through the same stages as the year-long sessions

        (2) Each group will begin with "What do you want to talk about today?"

        (3) Each group will end with "How do you think group went and how did you do?"

    c. Group goes through these phases at different rates of speed depending on

        (1) Group members

        (2) Member to member interaction

        (3) Sociology of the group as a whole

6. See RAPP script (Sample 12, Script for RAPP—Long Version, and Sample 13, Script for RAPP—Short Version, in Sample Materials Section of this book)

E. After RAPP, Share Experiences

1. Self-disclose feeling about the group

   a. Ask for questions, thoughts, feelings from group members

   b. Share your own thoughts with them

   c. All have a fear of losing ourselves in the group—that is the anxiety we are experiencing right now

   d. Try to elicit what the members are experiencing

      (1) Pictures that come to mind

      (2) "A penny for your thoughts"

      (3) Sometimes leader can model by sharing own thoughts

2. Share with group members the positive aspects of being in group

   a. Enjoyable—like a club

   b. Support system

   c. Learn to know yourself better

   d. Learn to tell people what you think and feel

   e. Learn to be open and honest

   f. Safe place to work through problems

   g. Place to make new and better friends

3. Leader will be less and less active as group develops

   a. Their group, not yours

   b. Not leader responsibility to "entertain" them

F. Third Group Session

1. Repeat RAPP

   a. Shortened version—summary

   b. Have them participate in summarizing

2. Hook to start discussion

   a. "What did you think about last week's group?"

   b. Dwell on feelings—begin to create awareness, but don't harp

3. You might begin with a format they are comfortable with

   a. Question and answer

   b. "Does anybody else feel that way?"

4. Avoid "going around the circle" to get each person to answer

   a. Creates anxiety about "their turn to talk"

   b. Not listening to person speaking

5. Do not "call on" anyone by name

VIII

MAINTAIN CONTROL AND PROVIDE PROTECTION
TASK TWO

A. GROUP MUST IDENTIFY WITH LEADER

1. Be the ego of the group

    a   Keep group under control

    b. Keep "law and order" at all times

    c. Keep group going in proper directions

        (1) From distrust into integration

        (2) From integration to working

        (3) Elicit appropriate behaviors for each stage

    d. There are many varied ways to get through these stages—do not lose sight of the goal

2. Be in control of the group, but not an authority figure

    a. If you walk into the group thinking, "I hope they behave today" or "I hope John is absent,"

        (1) The group is in control

        (2) Especially important in early adolescent groups

    b. Early adolescents need a tight rein like a horse

        (1) Does not mean you need to be loud, mean and/or physical

        (2) Invisible yet knowable line which may not be crossed

        (3) Adolescents want and need to be guided

        (4) Failure to establish this line will result in problems with group control and progress

3. Do not be an equal

    a. Be parental but not a parent

    b. Be friendly but not a friend

    c. Be a participant and observer

        (1) The more observation and less participation, the better the group will function

        (2) Group will be forced to take responsibility for own behavior

    d. Especially true in school setting

4. Leader has different function in group than classroom

    a. For students to feel free to air feelings not appropriately shared in school, leader must be perceived as having a different function in group setting

    b. Role of group leader must be isolated from other roles within school

5. Therapeutic leverage

    a. Maintains control and mastery

    b. Guarantees safety for members

    c. Never be perceived as giving up control of group

        (1) Golden Rule: "He who has the gold makes the rules"

        (2) May need to invoke, "Why? Because I said so."

            (a) Being too friendly severely hampers your ability to keep therapeutic leverage

            (b) It may be necessary later on to guarantee protection for a group members

6. Encourage maximum group self-direction

    a. Do not control group and solve all their problems

    b. Only invoke Golden Rule when **absolutely** necessary

    c. Use therapeutic leverage too often and it loses effectiveness

        (1) "I've heard this one before"

        (2) "Teacher—deaf"

        (3) Abuse it and you lose it

7. Guarantee safety

    a. Protection of member from

        (1) Scapegoating

        (2) Heavy focus (if necessary)

    b. Need to "stop action"

        (1) Confrontive: "Stop—don't do that!"

        (2) Subtle: "I really don't think this is being helpful"

        (3) Teach differences between

            (a) Dumping

            (b) Being cruel

            (c) Constructive criticism

    c. Give opinions as opposed to making authoritarian statements; bigger payoff in the long run

B. PROVIDE AND MAINTAIN THERAPEUTIC ENVIRONMENT OF GROUP

1. Demonstrate experience and knowledge

    a. Share experience

    b. Teach expectations

    c. Must establish self as "expert"

    d. Be the type of role model the students expect

    e. Give them direction

2. Predict problems

    a. Anticipate situations

    b. 7 "P's" (proper prior planning prevents pitifully poor performance)

        (1) The more you can anticipate problems, the better you respond to them

    c. Predicting future events is beneficial

        (1) Increases group cohesiveness

        (2) Gives credibility to leader

        (3) Establishes therapeutic environment

3. Give validity to norms

    a. Model appropriate behavior

        (1) Give positive feedback for appropriate on-task behaviors

        (2) Teach members how group should function

        (3) When seeing group function appropriately, reinforcing it will help maintain a proper therapeutic environment

    b. Use the information in the summary notes to further reinforce for next group

    c. Group counseling is a process, not an event

        (1) It takes time, modeling and going through the process to generate any desired outcome

        (2) Building a Bridge (Analogy)

            You lay the foundation in the ***distrust stage.*** You teach the group members which way the traffic flows in the ***integration stage.*** If you rush them through this process, they will fall off the bridge into the water. But, if you wait until the span of the bridge is completed, in the **working stage,** then the group will go across the bridge and be a functional group. It is important that the group leader be patient enough to go through the entire process, and not push for greater speed of completion.

You plant seed in the Fall to harvest in the Spring.

4. Protect right of individual to work on problems in the group and to use group beneficially

   a. Move group from off-task to on-task behavior

   b. It is the right of any member to pursue a topic if he chooses

      (1) Leader's task to help group focus, listen, and allow that person to work

      (2) "It seems like Mary would like to talk about this"

      (3) Leader may also assist a student in bringing up a particular topic

   c. Focus on the feelings and reasons behind the action, rather than the actual event

      (1) "Khaddafi Story"

      If a member brings up Khaddafi and the military intervention that took place, direct them toward his behavior; 'some people may do things that don't make a lot of sense'; or, 'people sometimes do really crazy things'. See if the group will respond. You don't address the issue of off-task behavior in a direct manner, but use the verbalization as fuel to move someone into discussing feelings rather than non-personal issues. This is shaping through role-modeling, rather than direct intervention.

      (2) Real Issues—"I'm scared when people act in a way I don't understand"

   d. Being off-task in distrust stage is common

      (1) Do not shut anyone down

      (2) In this stage the process is more important than the content

         (a) Be glad members are talking and listening

         (b) Let them learn appropriate behaviors

   e. Skipping from topic to topic in integration stage

      (1) Typical of this stage; to be expected

      (2) May be current events, local sports information, or other irrelevant material

      (3) Avoid the superfluous and extraneous—reinforce any members that attempt appropriate group topics

   f. Skipping from topic to topic in the working stage

      (1) A form of resistance in this stage

(2) Leader very active and direct "What's that got to do with group?"

(3) May need to be even more direct, if above does not work

(4) Realize that the group will regress slightly, if leader uses a very direct intervention strategy

    (a) Members will be more hesitant to speak

    (b) Afraid that they aren't saying "what the leader wants them to say"

    (c) Use this direct, confrontive intervention only to provide protection of the right of a member to speak and be listened to

g. If the leader has to, he may choose to sacrifice an individual for the good of the group

    (1) Know when to focus on one student's problem to the exclusion of the group

    (2) Protect the group environment

h. Monopolizer

    (1) Shut him down

    (2) Provide him with information on his behavior and its effect on the group

        (a) "How is the group responding to what you are saying?"

        (b) Ask the group, and if you get no response, "How come no one is responding to you?"

        (c) Point out the others' reactions to him

        (d) Try to get the others to express the fact that they are bored, angry, or not interested

    (3) Monpolizer is also a group problem

        (a) Group gives tacit consent by not confronting behavior

        (b) Form of resistance and self-defense

        (c) Leader can choose to share this line of reasoning with the group to get a group reaction

            1. Self-reflecting loop

    (4) Leader has option to deal with monopolizer in either or both of the above methods

5. Protect individual's right to disclose issue even if group wants to ignore or avoid it

    a. Members may feel too threatened by topic on the floor

(1) Not wish to discuss it

(2) Fear of getting involved

(3) Too sensitive or scary

b. Group may be very resistant and exhibit many "diversionary" behaviors

(1) Leader must insure that the individual be heard

(2) Must protect right to talk

6. Protect individual's right not to discuss "an incident"

a. e.g., Pregnancy, trouble with police, etc.

b. Give student choice

(1) If you know about it, probably most of the group will know

(2) Provide opportunity, but don't force a discussion

(3) Some situations are **not** appropriate for the group to discuss

(4) Leader must handle it in a delicate and sensitive manner

(5) Other members will be waiting to take their cue from leader as to whether the issue will be addressed

(a) Group may be very silent at onset, waiting for leader to give permission to discuss the event

(b) Role is to provide guidance for group, while protecting the individual

(c) Never avoid issue entirely; acknowledge it indirectly, "Had a rough weekend, Tom?" and give individual the choice to pursue or drop

(d) See the following example

On a Friday night a student has a DUI, and is arrested. He is out on bail and back in school on Monday. He is a member of your group, and in Tuesday's group is present. Your comment as a group leader, once you get through "What do you want to talk about today?"; (there will, of course be a little bit of silence) might be to look at that person directly and say "Had a rough weekend, didn't you?" By doing that, you inform the student that you know. It also says; "It is up to you to comment." The member, at that point, has the choice to share with the group as much or as little information as he would like to. If he just goes "Uh-huh," and acknowledges your comment, but does not go any further, then it is clear that he does not want to talk about it. At that point, you can let it drop. If he follows up on your lead and does want to discuss it, then he is taking the initiative, and you have provided the opportunity for him to talk about it, share his concerns, or ask for help from the group. It is important when providing that opportunity to help the students get started in the discussion by, in essence, "giving them permission" to discuss the incident.

    (e) Important to discuss the feelings about the incident, rather than the actual fact

        [1] Not a "fact-finding mission" to gossip more accurately

        [2] Processing the feelings involved can be very beneficial for entire group not just person involved

c. Provides invitation for person to speak

    (1) Student's option to discuss or not

    (2) Leader protects right of choice

d. Group may or may not wish to take up discussion

    (1) If they are comfortable, they'll ask questions

    (2) If uncomfortable, they'll move away from the topic

    (3) Leader's discretion whether or not to continue

    (4) "The ego of the group is greater than the sum of its parts"

        (a) The group will only go as far as they are willing and then will refuse to go deeper; may begin clowning, joking, or otherwise misbehaving

f. Example

A young man's mother died from cancer over Christmas. It was certainly not unexpected, as she had been ill for a long period of time. But when members came back from Christmas, it was the role of the group leader to make a statement, such as, "I'm very sorry to hear about the death of your mother." By expressing condolences, the leader gives the opportunity for that boy to either talk about the situation or not. I think that you cannot avoid making a comment in that situation because, at a minimum, you must share your own feelings and model appropriate behavior for the group. On the other hand, to beg him to speak about it when he might not be ready, would be inappropriate and very detrimental, not only to the child, but would also make the group regress significantly as well.

7. Material disclosed outside the group to the leader ("spilling in your ear")

a. May take two forms

    (1) Very personal and crucial

        (a) Sexual or physical abuse

        (b) Drugs, alcohol

        (c) Suicidal potential

(2) Personal and not crucial

    (a) Difficulty with a math teacher

    (b) Break-up with boyfriend

b. Depending on nature of disclosure, the leader has 3 options

    (1) To direct the child to the guidance counselor—as group is not exempt from state and federal laws, regarding abuse and neglect cases, etc. (See section on Confidentiality p. 48)

    (2) Leader may have student save the information until group (non-crucial) as "grist for the mill"

    (3) Leader may choose to handle issue personally

        (a) If it goes beyond leader's skill level, go with child to counselor for help

c. Hopefully, it will also surface in the group discussion at a later date.

8. When the "spilling in your ear" is about someone other than themselves

a. Not appropriate

b. Causes group to lose effectiveness

c. Turn it back to the group

    (1) "Why don't you bring that to group?"

    (2) Process this behavior with the group

d. If the "spilling" occurs frequently and by several members

    (1) Appropriate for leader to address it in group

    (2) Stress that the information belongs *in* group

    (3) Stress the need to trust each other

    (4) Stress that sharing *in* the group develops cohesiveness

e. "Spilling" will occur most often at end of group session

    (1) While leader is walking down hall to next class

    (2) Information is most immediate in their minds

    (3) Leader and secondary leader should exit together, to minimize "spilling"

    (4) "Spilling" is sometimes due to student's desire to be special to the leader

    (a) The leader is special to them

    (b) Foster equality between all group members by not permitting "spilling" at that time

    (c) Avoids "leader's pet" image

    (d) Allowing "spilling" at the end of group creates sibling rivalry

    (e) Creates splitting of group members that will cause significant problems later on

    (f) Will result in decreased effectiveness of the group process

9. Group is a primary prevention project and is very beneficial in identifying students who may need individual help

    a. More efficient use of counselor's time

    b. Increases identification of possible "over-looked" problem cases

    c. Creates a greater caseload for counselor, but saves a lot of the "investigative" time when a child comes to a counselor with a problem already identified and wanting to talk about it

10. Additional note: If a crucial situation is brought up in group

    a. Leader goes to that member outside group and expresses deep concern about disclosure—then must suggest that they go **together** to see the counselor about it

        (1) Do not **send** the child; rather accompany him or her

        (2) The member would not share the information in group if they were not ready

        (3) Not a breech of confidentiality rule, because you are going with them

        (4) Fulfilling your legal and moral obligation

C. SET PROTECTIVE LIMITS THEN

1. Defiance and antagonism usually mask fears

    a. A sign that one or more group members feel very vulnerable

    b. Manifests in some type of negative, resistant behavior

    c. Normal

    d. Adolescents act-out when feeling

        (1) Lonely

        (2) Scared

        (3) Frightened

    e. Feeling triangle

2. Limits on acceptable behavior

    a. Stop unacceptable behavior

        (1) If only one member, extinguish before alliance is formed, resulting in a collective resistant and defense

    b. Usually can be handled by letting the group back off of the subject being discussed and begin again on another topic or issue

3. Maintain external boundaries and control

    a. Leader must ascertain whether inappropriate behavior is

        (1) Deliberate act

            (a) Purely attention getting

            (b) Jokes, fall off chair, etc.

            (c) Done to sabotage the group

        (2) Function of emotional difficulties

            (a) Part of that child's "normal" behavior

            (b) Caused by emotional problems and individual needs

    b. Bizarre behavior in group

        (1) Do not lecture or attack directly

(a) Other members will coalesce to member's defense

(b) Leader appears to be unsympathetic

(2) Do not ignore

   (a) Makes mockery of the group

   (b) Members will not let you get away with it

   (c) Harms leader's credibility

(3) Must "control"

   (a) Acknowledge behavior, but don't be confrontive or judgmental

   (b) Avoid creating a power issue

      [1] "Billy, what you're doing doesn't make sense to me"

      [2] Turn to group and say, in a non-threatening tone, "Does that bother anyone else besides me?", then let it drop, the group will take it further if they choose

   (c) If you are sitting close enough, just putting your hand on the distracting student, or look at that person, a shake of your head and frown may stop the behavior

      [1] Try to do these non-verbal techniques in a subtle way, without breaking the flow of the group

      [2] Leading a group is like conducting a orchestra; don't stop the music while handling a disruption

c. If someone leaves group

   (1) In the middle of a session, or permanently due to moving from the area (termination)

      (a) Group should process the termination immediately

      (b) Do not let the group discuss the person or the event after the person has left

      (c) Group will think "When I leave the group they will talk about me."

   (2) Focus on how members feel about the event at the time it occurs

      (a) Anger at person for "quitting" on them

      (b) Protection of confidentiality rule

      (c) Guilt feelings—"Was it something I said?"

   (3) Maintain protective boundary

      (a) See the following example:

A girl we will call Teresa was a patient on an adolescent mental health unit for 75 days. She had a very rough life, leaving home in part because her mother had thrown her out of the house. Throughout her stay on the unit, she was talking about being different, standing up for herself and being more assertive. One of the things she said was that under no circumstances would she ever return to live with her mother. After being on the unit for 75 days, Teresa's mother finally showed up for the very first time and Teresa left that night, against medical advice, with her. The next day in the group everyone wanted to talk about Teresa and what had happened. The leaders did not allow the members to talk about Teresa at all, but instead provided the opportunity for them to talk about their feelings about Teresa leaving. They were very angry because "she didn't practice what she preached"; they had "wasted a lot of time" in group giving her advice, which obviously, she had not taken. They also felt very guilty, feeling like maybe they should have kept Teresa's mother away from her or said something to Teresa that night to keep her from going. They were also wondering if they had done something wrong and made her leave so suddenly. For group to be beneficial and also to protect Teresa (and everyone else who might ever miss or leave the group), all of those feelings must be processed. It was not important to talk about Teresa herself or the events of the night before; rather, the focus had to be the anger and the guilt feelings of the group members. Process the feelings rather than the event.

4. Be a protector, not a policeman

   a. Do not make yourself responsible for every outside behavior of your group members

   b. Do not confront students with misbehaviors which occur outside the group

      (1) Increases defenses

      (2) Increases resistance

      (3) Decreases group involvement

   c. Tell the teacher who brought you the outside problem

      (1) You appreciate the information, but you cannot bring it to group

         (a) Protects the student's rights

         (b) Maintains integrity of group

5. Differentiate heavy focus from scapegoating

   a. Scapegoating—"picking on" a member

      (1) Judgmental and angry

      (2) Displacement reaction by members

      (3) Starts out trying to be helpful but goes too far, gets carried away or loses sight of original objective

(4) May really be angry at leader

(5) A way to keep focus off themselves

(6) Causes target member to feel badly

(7) Leader must rescue (protect) the scapegoat

    (a) "I don't think this is being very helpful."

    (b) Remind them of the difference between constructive criticism and "dumping" and/or being cruel

    (c) May even need to totally stop the process and begin again

b. Scapegoating is a form of group resistance

(1) Receptacle for conflict in the group

(2) Acting-out behavior which is "grist for the mill"

c. Heavy focus

(1) Non-judgmental

(2) (Insight) x (Action) = Change

    (a) If you multiply something by nothing, you get nothing

(3) A sincere attempt to be helpful, by giving the target member feedback about how he is perceived by others or why he does what he does

(4) Uncomfortable for member, but not harmful an attempt to help that person change

(5) Done with a more even-leveled mood and with more group participation

(6) Very beneficial allow it to occur; facilitate it, reinforce appropriate group behavior

D. MAINTAIN AND PROTECT RULES

1. Rules need not be extensive

   a. Three main rules of RAPP

   b. Also additional rules which develop as the group develops

   c. All school rules must be enforced because group is a class and a part of school

2. Must be clear, concise and easily enforced

3. Violation of the rules are a violation of the boundaries and structure of group

   a. Individual issue

   b. Also a group issue

   (1) Feelings are put into action

   c. e.g., Coming to group on drugs and/or alcohol

   d. e.g., Coming late to group

4. Leader sets the standards

   a. Be authoritarian enough to insure group is a safe place to share

   b. Be active

   (1) "Non-directive, passive leadership creates ambiguity, increases anxiety"

   (2) Groups in the ***Adolescent Group Counseling in Schools Project*** are not Rogerian

   (3) "Float like a butterfly, sting like a bee"

   c. Easy to be strict at first, then reduce strength and control as group develops

   (1) Better to have control and relinquish it than try to obtain control once it has gotten away

5. Must be careful not to establish precedent that leader will resolve group problems

   a. Encourages dependency, thus creating more anxiety and group resistance

   b. Their group, not yours—their responsibility to work, not yours

6. Testing confidentiality

   a. Most important rule

b. It will be tested—expect it; anticipate dealing with it

    (1) Biggest fear from faculty and staff in a school group

    (2) Easy to resolve

    (3) "Grist" for the mill

c. Members find out "who shares what with whom"

d. Key issue of group—trust

    (1) It's usually teachers and not students who break confidentiality

    (2) When you give the students the responsibility for their own group, they take it and protect it

e. The most underestimated, and under-utilized resources in schools are students

f. Leaders need to keep the rule themselves and have faith

g. The group will deal with any breech in confidentiality

    (1) Only insignificant information is leaked out to test the rule

    (2) Usually very early in the group year

    (3) Usually only happens once, if at all, just to test

    (4) Once dealt with, serves to strengthen the cohesiveness of the group

FACILITATE PROCESSING OF THOUGHTS AND FEELINGS-TASK THREE

A. HELP THE GROUP MEMBERS BECOME ALLIES

1. Promotes bonding and caring about each other

2. Decreases feeling of isolation

    a. Become a part of a group

    b. Share a common goal

B. GROUP MEMBERSHIP, ACCEPTANCE, AND APPROVAL ARE ESSENTIAL TO SUCCESSFUL OUTCOME

1. An open and honest atmosphere must develop

    a. Honest feedback is very beneficial

    b. When you are giving advice to others, you are also receiving advice yourself

    c. When you receive advice, you also help the person who gives it

2. The adolescent's need for support must be recognized

3. Unconditional acceptance must be present

C. THE GROUP MUST ACHIEVE AUTONOMY AND SELF-RESPECT

D. THE GROUP BECOMES THE "AGENT" OF CHANGE

1. The group has to believe that if a change for the better is to occur, the members must bring it about themselves

2. Process becomes important

   a. Vehicle to examine personal issues

3. Group provides the common stimulus

   a. Each person reacts differently to that stimulus based on own personal dynamics

4. The role of "facilitator" (group leader) is not the way teachers are typically seen by students

   a. Teachers seen as "dispensers of knowledge"

      (1) "Teach me and I'll learn"

      (2) Not "show me the way and I'll teach myself"

   b. Also changes the way teachers perceive themselves

E. THE LEADER AND THE GROUP MEMBERS MUST DEVELOP MUTUALLY AGREED UPON GOALS

1. Keeps group on course

2. Helps determine appropriate intervention strategies

3. Allows evaluation of group progress

F. GROUP NORMS MUST DEVELOP

1. The role of the leader is to set and shape group norms

    a. Give recognition to "norms" established by the group as the group develops

        (1) Explicit

        (2) Implicit

    b. Norms that foster group growth

        (1) Feedback—teach group members how to give and receive it

            (a) Specific and direct

            (b) Non-judgmental

            (c) Timely

            (d) Personal

        (2) Risk-taking

        (3) Confidentiality

        (4) Openness

        (5) Honesty

    c. Discourage

        (1) Taking turns talking

        (2) Leader centered group—their opinion, not yours

        (3) Outside material

        (4) "Crisis intervention" approach

        (5) Advice giving

2. Norms help members feel part of and committed to the group

    a. Group members don't solve problems as much as they give suggestions and facilitate change

    b. Most people don't (won't) take advice

3. Norms offer stability a "constant" in a "variable" experience

G. CURATIVE FACTORS MUST DEVELOP

Yalom cites eleven (11) curative factors that help students who participate in group psycho-therapy [Yalom, I.D. (1985). *The Theory and Practice of Group Psychotherapy,* pp. 3-104. New York: Basic Books.]

1. Instillation of hope

   a. Things are not hopeless, they can get better

2. Universality—"you are not alone"

3. Education and clarification—the imparting of information

   a. Literally teach group members information

      (1) Venereal disease, pregnancy, drugs, etc.

   b. Members give lots of advice to others as a means of self-defense

4. Ventilation and sharing

   a. Group members will vent feelings

      (1) Parents drinking

      (2) Divorce

      (3) A sibling's inappropriate choice of mate

5. Developing social skills

   a. Model leader

   b. Model other "healthier" adolescents

   c. Improve interpersonal skills—how to get along with others

   d. Learn value of helping others

6. Insight into the "why's" of the students problems

   a. Insight into personal behavior and how it is perceived by others

   b. How members' behavior affects others and vice versa

   c. Why they do what they do (personal insight)

d. Help students understand their antecedents—how they got to be the way they are

   (1) "Shame on your parents for the way you are today—but shame on **you** if you stay that way"

7. The above "curative factors" come in and out of play during the life of a counseling group

H. ACTIVITY—CURATIVE FACTORS IN GROUP (See Sample 16 in Sample Material Section of this book)

I. GROUP COHESIVENESS—MOST SIGNIFICANT CURATIVE FACTOR

[Yalom, I. D. (1985). *The Theory and Practice of Group Psychotherapy,* pp. 48-56. New York: Basic Books.]

1. Cohesiveness-the attraction that members have for each other and for the group

2. Members of cohesive groups are more accepting of one another, more supportive, more inclined to form meaningful relationships in the group

3. When a group develops cohesiveness it has become a group

   a. The members will demonstrate to each other

      (1) Concern

      (2) Acceptance

      (3) Genuineness

      (4) Empathy

      (5) Sensitivity

      (6) Reassurance

      (7) Helpfulness

      (8) Connectedness

   b. Helps maintain and achieve group goals

   c. Increases conformity to group norms

4. Another definition of cohesiveness

   a. The movement of the transference relationship from the leader to the group members

5. Goal of group leader is to get the transference relationship to go from member-to-leader to member-to-member interaction

a. Students come to group seeing leader as the savior and cure-all, the one to impress and win

b. Move them from the leader doing the work, to the group doing the work

    (1) They should care more about interacting with each other than with the leaders

    (2) They should worry more about each other than about the leaders

c. When this occurs, the members can do the work of the group

6. Transference in groups

a. May not only be with the leaders, but can and should be with members

b. Very powerful if members can see and point out transference relationships to each other

c. Leader must give feedback to the members regarding the distortion, "I'm a little confused why you are so angry with me."

7. Teenagers use group as "testing grounds"

a. They try out in group what they would like to do in future relationships (transitional object)

    (1) e.g., will practice confronting Dad in group (leader) before going home and actually confronting Dad

J. FUNCTIONS OF THE LEADER TO FACILITATE THE GROUP'S MOVEMENT FROM COGNITIVE MATERIAL TO AFFECTIVE MATERIAL (GOING FROM WHAT YOU THINK TO HOW YOU FEEL)

1. Cognitive/Affective ratio

2. The leader becomes the instrument for this transition

    a. Leader must generate emotions

        (1) Directly

        (2) Through sarcasm

        (3) With humor

        (4) By accurately labeling behavior

3. Attempt to generate anger at the leader

    a. "Stir the pot"

    b. Confront

4. Look for theme

    a. e.g., Substance abuse, feelings about parents, teachers

    b. Feed them

        (1) Tasks to generate talking about feelings

        (2) "Anybody else feel this way?"

5. Job is to generate feelings, get out of the way, and let the group process it

    a. Four possible feelings

        (1) Happy

        (2) Sad

        (3) Fear

        (4) Anger

    b. Anger is the easiest to deal with

        (1) It is easiest to show the underlying causes are either sadness or fear

        (2) Like an iceberg, most of it lies beneath the surface

        (3) Feeling triangle

  c. When generating anger, try directing them to discuss the underlying reasons

        (1) The more the leader can pinpoint the cause of the anger, the more clearly the problem can be interpreted

6. Help members be specific

  a. Feelings

  b. Problems

  c. Solutions

  d. See Sample 1, "Thoughts for Adolescents and Others to Live By," in Sample Materials Section of this book

7. Whenever possible, always shift from cognitive to affective mode

  a. "I know what you think, but how do you feel about it?"

  b. Delve deeper than just surface feelings—get to the core issue which is usually the fear of growing up

K. RESISTANCE

1. Any behavior that moves the group away from areas causing discomfort

   a. Heavy focus

   b. Sensitive/controversial

   c. Personal issues

2. Reason for resistance

   a. Lack of trust

      (1) Fear of talking

      (2) Fear of response

      (3) Fear break in confidentiality

   b. Anger

   c. Control of

      (1) Self—loss of control—scared of saying something "stupid" or offensive

      (2) Group—control, i.e., power

   d. Hopelessness

   e. "I don't want to be here and I am angry"

3. May take the form of

   a. Withdrawal—silence

   b. Defensive body language

   c. Intellectualization—"shallow brooks are noisy"

   d. Hostility toward

      (1) Leader

      (2) Other member

      (3) Depends on member's own dynamics

         (a) Having problems with parents—project to leader

         (b) Problems with siblings—project to peers

(4) Better to have member project to the leader who can probably handle it better

e. Lack of productive work

    (1) "How many psychologists does it take to change a light bulb?"

    (2) Non-significant issues

        (a) Friday night's basketball game

        (b) Price of tea in China

        (c) Changing the subject

4. May occur early and/or late in the group process

a. If early-usually issue of trust

b. If later-usually issue of discomfort

c. If the leader makes the group uncomfortable—you are doing a good job

    (1) If they are squirming, they are thinking

d. Resistance and anger are the "meat" of group change and growth

5. Must be overcome for group to move on

a. Try to focus on process (what is taking place)

    (1) "John is really shooting the breeze"

    (2) "Mary just wants to work on others, not herself"

b. Avoid interpreting to the group—creates leader dependence

c. Do not let members place the responsibility on leader

    (1) Put the focus back on them

    (2) "Let's work on everyone else's problems but mine"

d. Do not let them scapegoat

    (1) The group will pick the most vulnerable member to work on

e. Try to wait them out if silent

    (1) Most difficult for leader to deal with

f. As with other forms of resistance, try to work them through the process

g. Let the group do the work

6. When and if you choose to confront, tell group members

    a. "This is how group avoids work"

        (1) "Fights"—verbal or even physical

        (2) "Flight"—change the subject

        (3) "Dependency"—going silent and expecting leader to rescue them

L. STATEMENTS THAT CAN BE SAID IN GROUP TO FACILITATE THE PROCESSING OF THOUGHTS AND FEELINGS

1. Opening—"What do you want to talk about today?"

2. Closing—"How did group go and how did you do?"

3. "How do you feel about that?"

4. "Has anybody else had that problem?"

5. "Has anybody else felt that way?"

6. "How come?" rather than "why?"

   a. Puts members in a less defensive posture

7. You seem...angry, sad, etc.

   a. Non-judgmental

8. "I'm not really sure what you are saying."

   "Can you explain (or clarify) that?"

   "Can anybody help me?"

   "Is it that you can't follow it either?"

9. NOTE: 3-8 are good for secondary leader to use as well

   a. Bails leader out of trouble

   b. Keeps the group on-task while giving the leader time to regroup

M. TO BE SUCCESSFUL, FOCUS OF GROUP MUST BE ON

1. Relationships

2. "Here and Now" feelings

3. Cohesion

    a. Members think of themselves as a group

    b. Each member's contribution is valued

    c. Group works together toward

        (1) Each member's goals

        (2) Group goals

4. The responsibility for the group rests with the group members, not the leader

    a. "It is your group, not mine"

X

PROVIDE INSIGHT INTO PROBLEM BEHAVIOR
TASK FOUR

A. NOT AS IMPORTANT AS YOU WOULD IMAGINE—IF YOU NEVER GET TO IT, YOU WILL STILL HAVE AN EFFECTIVE GROUP

1. Advantage of the "here and now" approach

2. Interpersonal issues, not psychodynamic issues

B. BEYOND THE BEHAVIOR AND THE FEELING ASSOCIATED WITH THE EVENT, IT BECOMES IMPORTANT TO EXAMINE THE RAMIFICATIONS OF A PROBLEM BEHAVIOR

1. Teach them how their behavior affects other people

    a. "Are you aware that this is what people think about you?"

2. Immediate cause and effect

C. INTERPRETER OF UNCONSCIOUS THOUGHTS AND ACTIONS

1. Magical thinking of omnipotence of leader

    a. You have no crystal ball

2. Do not try to function as "The Brilliant Analyst"

3. Strong sense of authority...but "I don't have all the answers"

    a. "Don't tell me—tell them"

D. PROVIDE INSIGHT

1. Identify antecedents of behavior

2. Identify feelings

3. Help group member discover incongruities between thoughts and feelings

4. Help clarify how these feelings have come to occur

    a. Use of "I" messages

        (1) "I" + "the feeling" + "behavior causing it"

        (2) "I feel angry when you whisper during my lecture, because it distracts me"

        (3) Less confrontive—non-judgmental—decreases scapegoating

5. Help student understand how these feelings have caused difficulty in day-to-day functioning

    a. "When you laugh at people it hurts their feelings"

    b. The good group leader relates what happens *in* the group, to what is happening *outside* the group

6. Cannot underestimate importance of relating current interaction within the group of interpersonal problems outside

    a. Microcosm of a macrocosm

    b. "You don't have to tell me your problems, I'll observe them."

    c. Practice new insight in the group, the group members will later use these insights outside the group

7. Insight provided by member-to-member is *infinitely* more powerful than insight provided by the leader

E. INSIGHT NECESSARY BUT NOT SUFFICIENT FOR BEHAVIOR CHANGE

1. Just telling them "why they do what they do" is not sufficient to get the type of change desired

2. Must do something about what they learn

   a. (Insight) x (Action) = Change

      (1) Upon providing students with the insight, the leader must let them practice the new behavior in order to achieve change

      (2) If you multiply something by zero, you get nothing

3. Look for similarities within and among the group members to foster the "action"

   a. Universality

   b. "It's not just you who feels this way"

4. Group must follow through with insights provided to increase personal growth and group growth

   a. "Now what can we do about it?"

5. Group good place to practice insight learned

   a. Insight can be processed, channeled

   b. Group provides needed support to practice

   c. Additional benefit of helping, makes group feel better about itself

      (1) Increases cohesiveness

      (2) The more universal you make the experience, the more powerful it becomes

      (3) Increases individual member's self-esteem

6. Generalize individual insight to other group members

   a. Look for common link within the group

   b. Relate insight to events outside group

F. TIMING IS CRUCIAL

1. "Sense of timing" one of the most important skills

   a. Group is an apprenticeship trade

   b. Timing develops over years of experience

2. Really a group (developmental stage) factor as well as an individual factor

3. Key variables

   a. Readiness of each individual to share feelings

      (1) The opposite of love is not hate—but indifference

      (2) Leader must "read the clues"

   b. Level of defenses

      (1) The more obvious the defense, the more vulnerable the student—and the more need to deal with the issue

   c. Readiness to deal with material

   d. Degree of significance of material

      (1) Sometimes an issue won't be worth dealing with

      (2) If there are two important issues at the same time:

         (a) Deal first with the one that you are not likely to see again

         (b) Hold until later, the one which is most likely to reappear

         (c) Important issues will almost always reappear

4. Groups develop at different rates

   a. Giving insight is most beneficial in the working stage

   b. If insight occurs before this

      (1) It is hard to reference

      (2) It scares other group members

   c. Don't show off

      (1) "Just because you know your stuff, doesn't mean you need to flash it"

      (2) Patience is a virtue

(3) Therapy is a process—not an event

5. If moving too fast, group resistance will increase

    a. Disruptive behavior

    b. Jokes

    c. Silence

6. Members will tell leader to slow down

    a. "It seems like the group is not ready to discuss this; we will come back to it"

    b. Move to "safer" topic, if possible

    c. No harm done—just back off

    d. Therapeutic Guess

        (1) Three outcomes possible

            (a) Guess and be correct

            (b) Guess and be wrong—member will correct you

            (c) Guess and be wrong—member will say nothing about it

        (2) In two out of three—you win

7. Generalize to group as a whole before providing indepth insight to a particular member

    a. Going horizontally—as opposed to going vertically

    b. Vertically

        (1) Asking for more information

        (2) Digging deeper

        (3) Fact-finding mission

        (4) Normal human response but not beneficial for our purposes

    c. Horizontally

        (1) Concentrate on the feeling—not the fact

        (2) "It took courage for you to share that with us"—"I'm glad you felt comfortable enough to do it"

        (3) Sharing some items of great importance with the group shows trust, and bolsters the group's cohesiveness tremendously

d. Example: Significant Self-disclosure

A teen in your group tells the group that he is gay. The group is shocked and doesn't know how to deal with this information. Rather than ask him the "how-why-when" types of questions, the leader congratulates him for his courage and thanks him for his trust in the group. The leader praises the group for inspiring trust. Homosexuality is not the issue—the comfort with the group and being able to reveal that he is gay is. The member is really using the group to test reactions to his disclosure, before he goes out in the world to try it. Concentrate on the feelings; fear of rejection, bad treatment by others, rather than the facts.

8. Before offering any insight, wait 30 seconds

   a. A member of the group will probably say what you were going to say

   b. Much more powerful coming from another member than coming from the leader

9. After leader offers insight, group will usually regress

   a. Group stops working as momentarily members become leader dependent

   b. Don't get alarmed—expect it—look for it

   c. Group will move back through the phases again at a quicker pace

10. After a significant and intense group, the level of group intensity will lighten in the next session

   a. Level of feelings generated frighten group members for short time

   b. Members need room to breathe for a while

G. GENERAL THOUGHTS ON INTERVENTION

1. Intervention by the leader helps the group focus

2. Intervention will produce consequences in the group

   a. Could be positive or negative

   b. But will produce group growth (eventually)

3. In order to intervene, a leader must decide three things

   a. What's happening in group at this point?

   b. Is change necessary?

   c. What intervention will bring about that change?

4. When in doubt, do nothing

5. When it is best to intervene

   a. Difficulty with group function

      (1) A distraction/disruption interferes with the normal running of the group

   b. Unconstructive and/or repetitive material

      (1) Move the group along

   c. Material is not goal-directed

      (1) "What's that got to do with group?"

5. What to look for when deciding if an intervention is appropriate

   a. A change in the atmosphere of the group

   b. Change in the level of participation

H. GENERAL METHODS OF CREATING CHANGE

1. Use "I" messages

   a. "I really feel you guys are dumping on Bob"

   b. Direct—but not confrontive

2. A hook—a task to perform

   a. Used to end a prolonged silence (i.e., 2-3 week's worth)

      (1) "What would you like to be able to do better: cry when you want to, show anger when you feel it, or ask for a hug?"

      (2) "What would you like to change about your life?"

      (3) "What age would you like to be?"

      (4) "What's the hardest thing about growing up?"

   b. Do not use all of the above in the same session—one or two at most

   c. Physically change your position in the chair—lean forward, look serious, project your body into the circle

3. Not all interventions are successful, but usually promote group growth

   a. Members may be angry at leader

   b. Leader may have the wrong strategy

   c. Members may have made a pact outside of group not to talk

4. Treat it like a therapeutic guess

   a. If none of the "hooks" work, turn it back to them

   (1) "Well, nothing I've said has interested you—so what *are* you interested in?"

   (2) If still no reaction—sit back and wait it out

5. Don't intervene too often

   a. One of the best interventions is to do nothing

I. TYPES OF INTERVENTIONS

1. Feedback

    a. Facts without any form of interpretation

    b. Provides focus

    c. Especially important in early stages

    d. Modeling—the world won't end if you tell someone how you feel

    e. "Say what you mean, and mean what you say"

2. Clarification

    a. More direct form of feedback

    b. Focus attention to central issue or theme

        (1) Stop the action and clarify what is going on

    c. Summarize what has transpired

        (1) Content

        (2) Feeling

        (3) Process

    d. Analyze relationships

    e. Ask for clarification directly

3. Confrontation

    a. Strong, direct type of feedback

    b. Not negative or aggressive

    c. Confront material—not the person

        (1) "I like you—but I'm not happy with what you are doing"

4. Interpretation

    a. To facilitate understanding and provide insight

        (1) Therapeutic guess

b. Attempt to link past, to present, to future

c. Focus on maladaptive behavior

d. Use of therapeutic guess

   (1) If inaccurate, will not hurt

   (2) Point out reason (evidence) that helped to form that observation

   (3) Hope for correction

   (4) "Play your hunches"

e. Use of "Thoughts for Adolescents and Others to Live By" (See Sample 1, in Sample Materials Section of this book)

   (1) e.g., Blamer

      (a) "When you point the finger..."

      (b) "Shame on your parents for..."

   (2) Accepting responsibility for other's feelings

      (a) Wave Story

f. Always move from leader doing the work to group doing the work

   (1) Consensual validation—"How many of you feel the same way?"

   (2) Voting—"Who believes what was just said?"

   (3) Rating—"On a scale of 1 to 10, with 10 being John is angry and 1 being John is not angry, how would you rate John's anger?" Then go around the group.

g. With each successful interpretation, the ability of the leader to effectively manipulate the group to its highest therapeutic level is significantly increased

   (1) Individual counseling with a cheering section-vs-individual counseling with an audience

J. IF LEADER CHOOSES TO FOCUS ON DEFENSE MECHANISMS

1. Do not strip defenses away-work around them

   a. Defenses develop for a good reason

   b. Defenses serve a purpose for that group member

2. Do not shame a group member

   a. Retards development of the member

   b. Retards development of the group

3. The more emotional difficulties the adolescent has, the more basic the issues, the more primitive the defenses (hide face, turn back to circle—yell at someone)

4. Denial is most common adolescent defense

   a. Must undo denial to make significant changes

   b. "I don't know" (IDK)

      (1) "IDK, IDK" or "IDK, I don't want to tell you"

      (2) If "IDK, IDK"

         (a) Let it pass and reassure group member

         (b) Teachers group is safe and no one will be forced to disclose information

         (c) Brings denial to honest conscious level

         (d) How can the group help you?

      (3) If "IDK, I don't want to tell you"

         (a) Admits something is present

         (b) Chooses not to disclose

         (c) "That's okay, maybe some other time you'll feel comfortable"

5. Displacement (taking the feelings that you have, and putting them on to someone else)

   a. Anger in group beneficial

      (1) Not dangerous

b. Transference of anger to the group leader

    (1) Trial run

c. Move issue to real source

d. Ally with the symptom

    (1) Agree with a member who may be off base in what he is saying (the group is unwilling to confront this behavior), by concentrating your attentions on him to the exclusion of the others; the leader creates hostility in the rest of the group, a jealous desire to get involved (i.e., sibling rivalry)

    (2) You may never need to use this

    (3) Empathize with feeling

    (4) Anger is to fear as

        (a) Aspirin is to temperature

        (b) Antibiotic is to infection

    (5) Conflict to underlying issue

    (6) Most of the time, anger is a smoke screen for the real issue—fear or sadness

e. The "Feeling Triangle"

f. e.g., Joe E.—Adjustment disorder with mixed disturbance of emotions and conduct; and mixed substance abuse, episodic

    (1) Anger—mother—"She won't let me do anything"

    (2) Fear

        (a) No one to take care of me

        (b) Can't control my anger

        (c) Drug abuse like Dad

        (d) Real issue

            [1] Mom and Dad divorces

            [2] Mom won't take Dad back

            [3] Wants Mom and Dad together (Fantasy Family)

            [4] Really can't change the situation

g. e.g., Tom E. Diagnosis—Separation anxiety disorder

(1) Anger—

    (a) I don't want to grow up

(2) Fear

    (a) I'll never grow up

    (b) Can't control my temper

    (c) I'm crazy

(3) Real issue

    (a) Mom and Dad divorced

    (b) Sexually abused

    (c) Homosexual panic

h. Counter-dependent adolescent

(1) "Don't teach me anything that's different from what I already know—because I'm not sure of it"

    (a) The best defense is a good offense

    (b) Act tough

    (c) Attempt to "case-out the place"

    (d) Frequent in the distrust stage

(2) Power struggle for control of group

    (a) Member wants to run the group

    (b) Always show themselves early

    (c) Tests rules and the leader

    (d) Anything but what you want

    (e) Frequent in the integration stage

(3) Three ways for leader to cope with counter-dependent group member

    (a) In group invoke the "Golden Rule"

    (b) In individual session, process dynamics behind counter-dependency

    (c) In group process

[1] Acknowledge anger with empathy

[2] Reflect back to group (to gain support)

[3] Ask for feedback from the member and then the group (process the anger)

[4] Ask member and the group how they would like you to do it differently

    [a] Make the members to the work

    [b] Make the members take the responsibility to solve the problem

(4) Own personal agenda

  (a) Try to trap you into acting like their parents and/or teacher

  (b) Frame of reference becomes recapitulation of family dynamics

  (c) After issue of power and control is resolved

  (d) Frequent in the working stage

(5) Dependent Adolescent (Haut, 1988)

  (a) In the distrust stage

    [1] Close to leader

    [2] Talks about what the leader wants to talk about

  (b) In the integration stage

    [1] Scared

    [2] Tells parents "stuff" about group

      [a] Rapists and murders

      [b] "Waste of time"

  (c) In the working stage

    [1] Do not let them regress

    [2] Treat them if they are capable

(6) Do not work on individual but save the group

  (a) There comes a time to tell that member to be quiet and listen

(7) Interpret for benefit of the group

6. Yes...but game

   a. Guarantee it will occur

   b. Everything in front of the "but" is what the member thinks the group wants to hear—everything after the "but" is what that member really means

      (1) "Yes, I really want to go to group, but I don't have the time."

   c. Most common game in group

   d. Solicits advice, but rejects it

   e. Used to justify feelings of anger

   f. Helpless-rejection-complainer

   g. "No one understands me"

   h. Stay away from power battles

      (1) Don't confront directly

         (a) Generates more anger and "yes—but"

         (b) Lose—lose situation

   i. Banter—but do not mock

   j. Do not appear frustrated or resentful

   k. Can avoid most of this by discussing "Yes—But" early before there is an issue

      (1) It teaches the members to spot the game early and deal with it themselves, when it occurs later on

      (2) It generates support for the leader, when the leader deals with it later

NOTES

GROUP MEMBER'S BEHAVIORS

A. LEADER CREATES ENVIRONMENT OF GROUP BY THE WAY GROUP IS CONSTRUCTED AND HANDLED

B. BEHAVIOR INDIVIDUAL MEMBERS EXHIBIT IS A PRODUCT OF

1. Expectations of self and others

2. Personality factors

3. Characteristics of group (composition)

4. Characteristics of leader (personality, style)

C. THREE BASIC ELEMENTS IN EACH INDIVIDUAL TO EXPLORE

1. How member perceives and meets own needs [McClelland, D.C. (1967). **Personality.** New York: Holt, Rinehart and Winston.]

    a. Affirmation

        (1) Need to be liked, well-thought of, keep people happy

    b. Achievement

        (1) Goal oriented, need to be seen as competent

    c. Power

        (1) Impact and influence, need to persuade others

    d. Unmet needs motivate behavior

2. Interactional patterns among group members

    a. "I hate Mary, so I'll sit far away from her"

    b. "I really want to impress Bobby"

3. Relationship to the group as a whole

D. MEMBER'S BEHAVIOR MAY SERVE TO

1. Meet own needs solely

2. Facilitate the process of the group

3. Focus on the content

4. Help or hinder the functioning of the group

   a. Their role may be helpful to the leader, and/or the group—but not helpful for the individual member

5. Unmet needs motivate

   a. Key is to determine the actual need

E. HELPFUL TO IDENTIFY GROUP MEMBER'S BEHAVIOR AND ROLES (See Sample 19, Fishbowl Activity, in Sample Materials Section of this book)

1. Self-oriented

2. Task-oriented

3. Maintenance (process-oriented)

4. Manipulative

5. These behavior styles are never to be discussed during group—explained here as tool for primary and secondary leader's use only

F. SELF-ORIENTED BEHAVIORS

[Deutsch, M. (1960). The Effects of Cooperation and Competition Upon Group Process. In D. Cartwright and A. Zander (Eds.), *Group Dynamics Research and Theory.* Evanston, IL:, Row Peterson Co.]

1. Dominated by selfish interests over the group's interests

   a. Hinder group process

   b. Decreases building of cohesiveness

2. Dominator

   a. Motivation—power, achievement

   b. Tries to make all decisions

   c. Doesn't listen to others

   d. Tries to monopolize group

   e. Counter-dependent

3. Recluse

   a. Motivation—affiliation

   b. Withdrawn

   c. Makes little or no contribution

   d. Appears afraid to make a statement or express an opinion

   e. Wants to be liked

4. Aggressive blocker

   a. Motivation—power

   b. Counter-dependent

   c. Attacks others' remarks

   d. Quick to criticize

   e. Hostile and negative

   f. Seldom offers alternative ideas

5. Help-seeker

    a. Motivation—affiliation

    b. Low self-concept

    c. Asks others' opinion and advice

6. Recognition seeker

    a. Motivation-affiliation

    b. Tries to be center of attention

    c. Comments generally not on topic

    d. Similar to help-seeker, but not as focused

    e. "Yes—but" player

G. TASK-ORIENTED BEHAVIORS

[Deutsch, M. (1960). The Effects of Cooperation and Competition Upon Group Process. In D. Cartwright and A. Zander (Eds.), *Group Dynamics Research and Theory.* Evanston, IL: Row Peterson Co.]

1. Content oriented behaviors

   a. Keeps group moving

   b. Goals are consistent with leaders'

   c. Motivation fits all three identified needs; affiliation, achievement, power

   d. Helpful to a point—but too much is a problem

   e. May be doing it to keep focus off themselves

   f. Be aware if someone is in this role too consistently, or too often

   g. Form of avoidance

2. Initiator

   a. Motivation—affiliation, achievement, power

   b. Proposes tasks and/or goals

   c. Suggests solutions

3. Information seeker

   a. Motivation—affiliation, achievement, power

   b. Requests facts

   c. Seeks opinions

4. Information giver

   a. Motivation—affiliation, achievement, power

   b. Offers facts

   c. Expresses opinions

5. Clarifier

   a. Motivation—affiliation, achievement, power

b. Interprets ideas or suggestions

c. Indicates alternatives

6. Summarizer

a. Motivation—affiliation, achievement, power

b. Pulls together related ideas

c. Offers conclusions

d. Consensus taker

H. MAINTENANCE BEHAVIORS

[Deutsch, M. (1960). The Effects of Cooperation and Competition Upon Group Process. In D. Cartwright and A. Zander (Eds.), *Group Dynamics Research and Theory.* Evanston, IL: Row Peterson Co.]

1. Process oriented behaviors

    a. Used to help maintain a good working relationship among group members

    b. Motivation is primarily to keep group cohesive

    c. Rule keeper

    d. Uncomfortable with conflict, disruption or confusion

    e. Wants everyone to be happy

    f. The process is the product

2. Harmonizer

    a. Motivation—affiliation

    b. Peacemaker

    c. Reduces tension

3. Gatekeeper

    a. Motivation—achievement, affiliation

    b. Facilitator

    c. Keeps doors of communication open

4. Encourager

    a. Motivation—affiliation

    b. Friendly, warm, accepting

    c. Responder—verbal and non-verbal

5. Compromiser

    a. Motivation—affiliation

    b. Arbitrator

    c. Sacrifice own status in favor of group process

NOTES

OBSERVATION GUIDELINES FOR GROUPS

(See Sample 20, Observation Guidelines For Groups,
in the Sample Materials Section of this book)

A. TWO MAJOR AREAS TO OBSERVE—CONTENT AND PROCESS

1. Content (what's said in group)

    a. Subject matter or task orientation of the group

        (1) Past—"there and then"

        (2) Present—"here and now"

        (3) Future—"now and when"

    b. See Group Observation Checklist question (1)

    c. Keep content in "here and now" as much as possible

    d. Keep group "on task" as much as possible

2. Content—mainly facts or feelings

    a. Cognitive/affective ratio

    b. See Group Observation Checklist question (2)

3. Should strive for a balance between process and content, depending on the stage of the group (see later notes)

B. SPECIFIC AREAS OF PROCESS TO OBSERVE

1. Process

    a. What is happening among, between, and to group members

    b. Sensitivity to process helps leaders diagnose group problems early

        (1) If leader can figure out dynamics of the group, leader can usually "beat them to the punch"

2. Participation

    a. Who participates

    b. Frequency of participation

    c. Lack of participation

        (1) How are silent members treated

    d. Changes in participation

    e. Shifts in patterns of participation

    f. See Group Observation Checklist question (3)

    g. Active listening

        (1) Are they following the topics?

        (2) Are they listening while leader works on a specific issue?

        (3) If there are many different topics in a single group session, indicates that few members are listening

    h. See Group Observation Checklist question (4)

    i. Level of participation

        (1) Intensity

3. Atmosphere

    a. Tone, feelings, interests

    b. How involved are group members

    c. Working, passing time, hostile, cooperative

    d. Goal—open and accepting

e. Changes in atmosphere are most critical

   (1) Suppressed conflict

   (2) Unpleasant topics

f. Feelings and issues that are rarely discussed

   (1) Non-verbal messages

   (2) Facial expressions

   (3) Gestures

g. Learning to read the atmosphere helps leaders anticipate problems

h. See Group Observation Checklist question (8)

4. Membership

   a. Degree of acceptance by the group

   b. Inclusion, subgrouping, outcasts

5. Influence and power

   a. Struggle for group leadership

      (1) Struggle for power

      (2) Rivalry

   b. Leader must win the favor of the most powerful group members early

   c. Don't battle with the most powerful members

6. Decision-making

   a. Types of decisions

   b. Conflict resolution

   c. Methods of decision-making

      (1) By one

      (2) By minority

      (3) By majority without minority considerations

(4) By majority with minority considerations

(5) By consensus

d. Leader must **not** lose control of decision-making process

(1) Benevolent despot

(2) Golden rule—"He who has the gold, makes the rules"

7. Acceptance of structure

a. Norms

(1) Explicit

(2) Implicit

b. Achievement motivation

(1) Shared realistic goals

(2) Harmony in relationship to productivity

(a) Harmony—a group in which everyone agrees is generally non-productive

(b) Anger and resistance provide the impedance to productivity

c. Role and status within the group

d. If group is normally open and honest, but sudden changes indicate that something is wrong

(1) Exceptions: After an intense session

(2) Between weeks 15 and 20, when group resistance is down, and individual resistance is up

8. Key variables to observe in group members' behavior (See Sample 17, Development Stage, Group Behavior, and Its Effect on Leadership Style, in Sample Materials Section of this book)

a. Participation

(1) See Group Observation Checklist (Sample 20), questions 3 and 4

b. Anxiety

(1) See Group Observation Checklist (Sample 20), questions 5 and 6

c. Resistance

(1) See Group Observation Checklist (Sample 20), questions 7 and 8

d. Cohesiveness

(1) See Group Observation Checklist (Sample 20), questions 9 and 10

LEADERSHIP STYLE

A. WHAT CONSTITUTES GOOD LEADERSHIP STYLE IS NOT CLEARLY DEFINED

1. No theoretical or empirical proof that one leadership style better than another

2. Basic change process independent of theoretical orientation

B. IMPORTANT TO BECOME FAMILIAR WITH THE FOUR (4) DIFFERENT DIMENSIONS OF LEADERSHIP STYLE TO BE ABLE TO VARY DEPENDING ON

1. Leader's own needs

2. Needs of a particular group

3. Developmental stage of the group

C. LEADERSHIP STYLE BROKEN DOWN ALONG FOUR (4) BIPOLAR, INTER-DEPENDENT DIMENSIONS (Bednar and Stockton, 1980, and Rachmann, 1986)

1. Process—Content Orientation

   a. Process refers to "how" a particular issue is expressed by the group (what is actually going on)

      (1) Focus on communication and interaction patterns

      (2) Atmosphere, level of participation, decision-making, etc.

      (3) Methods of feedback and intervention

      (4) Emphasis on affective rather than cognitive material

   b. Content refers to "what" is said in the group

      (1) Reaction to "what is learned"

      (2) Clarifying information

      (3) Conveying factual information

      (4) Emphasis on cognitive rather than affective material

   c. Leader may choose to focus 100% on process—100% on content—or a combination of both

2. Subjective-Objective involvement (amount and degree of self-disclosure)

    a. Subjective involvement—the degree to which the leader is willing to be personally involved in the group (degree of self-disclosure)

        (1) Personal history—past, present, future

        (2) Feelings about the "here and now"

    b. Self-disclosure

        (1) Most helpful if focuses on feelings about the group (here and now)

        (2) Content of the group discussion

        (3) Personal history is less effective (sometimes necessary)

        (4) Difficult to say "how much" self-disclosure is best

        (5) When self-disclosure can be harmful

            (a) Do not self-disclose personal information that may be harmful

                [1] Did you ever do drugs?

                [2] Do you drink?

                [3] Were you a virgin when you got married?

            (b) Regardless of how you answer those questions you lose

                [1] If yes, you are a poor role model

                [2] If no, you are perceived as lying

            (c) Proper answer

                [1] How will that help you?

                [2] What does that have to do with your group?

    c. With objective involvement, the leader remains detached from the group

        (1) Interventions are limited to

            (a) Difficulties in group functioning

            (b) Re-focusing on process

            (c) Facilitating

        (2) Based on the belief that interventions made by group members are more potent than those made by the leader

    d. Activity—"Effective Use of Self-Disclosure" (See Sample 21 in Sample Materials Section of this book)

3. Individual—Group as a Whole Orientation

    a. Focus of leader's intervention toward an individual

        (1) Individual counseling with an audience

        (2) See diagram in Figure 2

Figure 2. Individual Orientation Model

        (3) Increases defenses of group members

        (4) Makes group leader-dependent

        (5) Increases transference material

    b. Focus of leader's interventions toward entire group

        (1) Process the process with group

        (2) Deal with "here and now"

        (3) More involved and exciting format

        (4) Offers better opportunity for members to learn about each other and themselves

        (5) Maximizes the potential of group

        (6) Fosters greater group independence

        (7) Encourages member to member interaction

        (8) See diagram in Figure 3

Figure 3. Group Orientation Model

(9) End results less important than how group gets there

(10) Horizontal vs. vertical interventions

(11) An example

    (a) A counter-dependent group member attacks the leader saying, "Group is worthless, I'm leaving"

    (b) If dealt with by leader

        [1] Paraphrase the anger

        [2] Encourage venting of feelings

        [3] Reflect "you seem frustrated and angry"

        [4] Relate to past "difficulty with authority figures"

        [5] Interpret "leaving is running from your problems"

    (c) If leader allows the members to work

        [1] Ask group members "Anyone else feel like this?"

        [2] "Is there something I am doing that is making you angry?"

        [3] Help clarify expectations

            [a] Whose group is it?

            [b] Who owns the problems?

        [4] How would you do it differently?

        [5] How do you deal with feelings toward authority figures who make you angry?

        [6] How do you feel when someone says "no" to you?

        [7] Builds group as vehicle to "solve" problems

c. Facilitating member-to-member interaction

    (1) Member talks to leader instead of addressing another member or entire group

        (a) "Tell them, not me"

    (2) Look at the floor

        (a) "Good eye contact" may not be good, as it creates dependence on leader

        (b) Avoiding eye contact avoids dependency

    (3) Use hand to motion the inclusion of the entire group

        (a) "Share with us all"

4. Empathy—Confrontation Intervention

   a. Empathy

      (1) Do not underestimate its value—counseling has its roots in empathy

      (2) Never lose with accurate empathy

      (3) Leader needs to listen and to teach listening skills

      (4) Best to learn to be understood and to understand

      (5) Avoid power struggles

      (6) Adolescents really do want to connect, in spite of behavior which appears contrary

      (7) When all else fails, go to empathy

   b. An interesting anecdote

      Empathy—A pastor told of visiting a family in a remote rural area. Arriving at the house, he was greeted by the mother, who said, "I just knew you'd stop in today! I need your help. I don't know what to do." She then told him about her problems, which brought tears to the pastor's eyes but were beyond his ability to solve. He didn't know what to say, so he continued to listen patiently until the woman, smiling through her tears, exclaimed, "Thanks for coming! This is exactly what I needed!" The minister commented, "Then I knew it was empathy, not wisdom, that she needed."

   c. Confrontation

      (1) Strong, direct type of feedback

      (2) Not negative nor aggressive

      (3) Confront material, not person

      (4) Use when conflict arises or to move group

         (a) Gets group's attention

      (5) Must be done with caring

      (6) Best done by group rather than by leader

D. AN EXAMPLE ILLUSTRATING ALL FOUR (4) DIMENSIONS OF LEADERSHIP STYLES

1. A group member has a "secret" to share with the group

2. The secret is shared

   a. How does the leader deal with "the disclosure"

   b. Vertical vs. horizontal interventions

NOTES

DEVELOPMENTAL STAGE, GROUP BEHAVIOR AND ITS EFFECT ON LEADERSHIP STYLE

(See Sample 17 in Sample Materials Section of this book)

A. DISTRUST STAGE (Sessions 1-6)

1. Dyad Technique—First Session

2. RAPP—second session

   a. Rules

   b. Approach

   c. Purpose

   d. Phases

3. Leader most active

   a. Establish procedures and rules

   b. Establish rationale

   c. Create expectations

   d. Predict problems

   e. "Set the stage"

      (1) Share values

      (2) Non-judgmental

      (3) Okay to express opinions

      (4) "Say what you mean and mean what you say"

4. Group behavior

    a. Participation—low

        (1) Members are strangers

        (2) Fear losing control

        (3) May be angry about being in group

    b. Anxiety—high

        (1) Threatening situation

        (2) Desire to make good impression

        (3) Lack clear understanding of what to expect

    c. Excitement

    d. Resistance—high

        (1) Distrustful

            (a) Leader

            (b) Each other

        (2) Hesitant to participate (fear of being "called on")

        (3) Anxiety

        (4) Test leader and each other

    d. Cohesiveness—low

        (1) Too early

        (2) Poor communication skills

        (3) Inadequate listening skills

5. Leadership style

    a. Content

        (1) Teach RAPP

    b. Process

        (1) Modeling

            (a) Communication skills

            (b) Listening skills

        (2) Teach members how to relate to each other

    c. Subjective

        (1) Fearful, anxious

        (2) Can disclose these feelings

            (a) Good Modeling

            (b) Decreases tension

        (3) "Here and now" disclosures only

        (4) Uneasiness with first group regardless of experience

        (5) Universality

            (a) "This is my first group, too, and I'm pretty scared"

    d. Group

        (1) Focus on constructing the group

        (2) Leader dependent

        (3) Will lose group if focus shifts to any one individual too soon

    e. Empathy

        (1) Anxiety reduction

        (2) Unconditional positive regard

        (3) Avoid anger response

        (4) Conflict must be avoided if at all possible

            (a) Throw it back to the group

B. INTEGRATION STAGE

(Sessions 6-15)

1. Group behavior

    a. Participation—gradually increases

        (1) Each group begins with silence

        (2) Moves to safe topics

            (a) School issues

            (b) Activities

            (c) Mostly negative

        (3) Advice giving

    b. Anxiety—moderate

        (1) Gradually decreases as trust develops

        (2) Participation itself serves to decrease anxiety

    c. Resistance—high

        (1) Individual resistance starts to decrease

        (2) Group resistance remains high

            (a) Intra-group conflict begins

                [1] Impatient with each other

                [2] Impatient with the process

                [3] Frequently off-task

                [4] Change subject—non-relevant material

            (b) Transferred to leader

                [1] Silence

                [2] Private conversations

                [3] Subgroupings

                [4] Outside group contact

                [5] Direct hostility

                [6] Antagonism

                [7] Testing of leader

d. Cohesiveness—developing

   (1) Bonding begins

   (2) Feelings expressed

      (a) Mostly negative

   (3) Norms are developing

      (a) Listening

      (b) Improved communication skills

      (c) Learning to give feedback

      (d) Disclosing honestly

   (4) Curative factors beginning

   (5) Confidentiality no longer a major concern

   (6) Less leader dependent

2. Leadership style

   a. Process is major emphasis, but move toward content

      (1) Less active

      (2) Shape group as a therapeutic system

      (3) Reinforce group's content discussions when on task

      (4) Actively facilitate processing of thoughts and feelings

         (a) Begins to move group from cognitive to affective material

      (5) Teach group members to be more specific

      (6) Shape norms through modeling

      (7) Protect the process

   b. Subjective

      (1) Reinforce curative factors as they develop

      (2) Self-disclose positive feelings as group increases in cohesiveness

   c. Group

      (1) Reflect antagonism back to the group

         (a) "Does everyone else feel that way?"

      (2) Encourage and support member to member interaction

      (3) Process advice giving

      (4) Leader should avoid giving advice

      (5) Do not focus on personal issues that surface

         (a) Choose horizontal over vertical interventions

      (6) Help group become agent of change

   d. Empathy

      (1) Listen empathetically

      (2) Clarify

      (3) Summarize

      (4) Stop just short of confrontation

C. WORKING STAGE

(Sessions 15-27)

1. Group behavior

   a. Participation—high

      (1) Less concerned about making good impression

      (2) Feedback honest and constructive

         (a) "Friend is someone who tells you what you need to hear, not what you want to hear"

      (3) Not afraid of losing control

      (4) Roles established and comfortable

   b. Anxiety—low

      (1) Safety in group

      (2) Ready to self-disclose personal issues

   c. Resistance—low

      (1) Group resistance is low

      (2) Optimistic and positive about the group experience

      (3) Individual resistance may be high as more personal and intimate material begins to surface

   d. Cohesiveness—very high

      (1) Intimacy has developed

      (2) Curative factors at work

      (3) Members are interdependent

2. Leadership style

   a. Content

      (1) Encourage maximum group self-direction

      (2) Use group to deal with underlying dynamics

      (3) Educate and impart information

      (4) Confront resistance

   b. Subjective

      (1) Can disclose personal issues if relevant

      (2) Can be an "expert"

   c. Individual and/or group

      (1) Therapeutic alliance established

      (2) Can take greater risks

      (3) Can intervene vertically if so desire

      (4) Can make mistake and group will support and/or rescue

      (5) Generate feelings and let the group do the work

      (6) Identification among members allows individual work

         (a) "Going around the room technique"

         (b) Voting and rating

      (7) Focus on defenses

         (a) Denial

         (b) Displacement

         (c) Projection

      (8) Provide insight and interpretation into underlying dynamics

         (a) Better if given by group members than by leaders

      (9) Allow group to be place to practice new behaviors

   d. Confrontation

      (1) Generate feelings through confrontation

(2) "Stir and pot"

(3) Confront—material not the person

(4) Differentiate between heavy focus and scapegoating

(5) Remember: The more confrontive the leader gets, and the more focus on the individual, the greater the risk

D. TERMINATION STAGE

(Sessions 28-30)

1. Group behavior

    a. Participation—high

        (1) Working through separation

        (2) Fear of loss of support

        (3) Fear of future

        (4) Fear of unknown

    b. Resistance—very low

        (1) May not want to leave

            (a) Regressed behavior

    c. Cohesiveness—very high

        (1) Therapeutic alliance

        (2) Intimacy

        (3) Strong bonding

        (4) Identification

        (5) Leader is not very important

2. Leadership style

   a. Process

      (1) Deal with feelings of intimacy

      (2) Process with group meaning of regressed behavior

   b. Subjective

      (1) Model sharing of feelings

         (a) Level of intimacy

         (b) Feelings of loss

         (c) Leader can self-disclose feelings of loss

   c. Individual

      (1) "Taking the chair"

         (a) A way to say good-bye

         (b) Last chance to give feedback

         (c) Is discussed in detail in Supervisory Session 7

      (2) Motivation to other, less successful members

      (3) Remind students of progress made

      (4) Encourage use of new skills and strengths

      (5) Counseling—"a process, not an event"

         (a) Encourage continued development of interpersonal skills

   d. Empathy and confrontation

      (1) Empathy regarding anxieties and fear of future, loss of support, etc.

      (2) Confront last chance to provide insight into problem behavior

NOTES

SELECTED BIBLIOGRAPHY ON
GROUP COUNSELING

Alonso, A. (1985). *The quiet profession—Supervisors of Psychotherapy.* New York, NY: Macmillan.

Anderson, N., & Marrone, T. (1977). *The program at number twenty-three.* Norristown, PA: Montgomery County Intermediate Unit.

Azima, F.J., & Richmond, L. (Eds.). (in preparation). *Adolescent group psychotherapy: AGPA monograph III.* New York: International Universities Press.

Bednar, R.L., & Stockton, R. (1980, November). *Training seminar of group leadership.* Presentation, Olgabey Park, W.V.

Bion, R.W. (1961). *Experiences in groups.* New York: Basic Books.

Brandes, N., & Gardner, R. (1973). *Group therapy for the adolescent.* New York: J. Arson.

Caplin, H.I., & Sadocak, B.J. (Eds.). (1971). *Comprehensive group psychotherapy.* Baltimore, MD: The Williams and Wilkins Co.

Corey, G. (1985). *Theory and practice of group counseling.* Monterey, CA: Brooks/Cole.

Corey, G., & Corey, M.S. (1987). *Groups: Process and practice.* Monterey, CA: Brooks/Cole.

Corey, G., Corey, M.S., Callanan, P.J., & Russell, J.M. (1982). *Techniques.* Monterey, CA: Brooks Cole.

Deutsch, M. (1960). The effects of cooperation and competition upon group process. In D. Cartwright and A. Zander (Eds.), *Group dynamics research and theory.* Evanston, IL: Row Peterson.

Durkin, H. (1964). *The group in depth.* New York: International Universities Press.

Hansen, J.C., Warner, R.W., & Smithe, E.J. (1980). *Group counseling theory and process.* Chicago, IL: Rand McNally.

Haut, S. (1988, February). *Adolescent group psychotherapy: A developmental perspective.* Presentation, New York, NY.

Kibel, H.D. (1981). A conceptual model for short-term inpatient group counseling. *American Journal of Psychiatry, 138:1,* 74-80.

Maxmen, J.S. (1978). An educative model for inpatient group therapy. *International Journal of Group Counseling, 28,* 2, 321-38.

McClelland, D.C. (1967). *Personality.* New York, NY: Holt, Rinehart, and Winston.

Meeks, John E. (1971). *The fragile alliance: An orientation to the outpatient psychotherapy of the adolescent.* Baltimore, MD: Williams and Wilkins Col.

Pfeiffer, J.W., & Jones, J.E. (1972, 1973, 1974, 1975, 1976, 1977, 1978, 1979). *Annual handbook for group facilitators.* Iowa City: University Associates.

Rachman, A.W. (1986, February 15). *The tough and tender roles of the adolescent group psychotherapist.* Presentation, Washington, DC, American Group Psychotherapy Association.

Rutan, J.S., & Stone, W.N. (1984). *Psychodynamic group psychotherapy.* Lexington, MA: The Collamore Press.

Siepker, B.B. & Kandaras, C.S. (1985). *Group therapy with children and adolescents: A treatment manual.* New York, NY: Human Sciences Press.

Shostram, E.L. (1967). *Man the manipulator: Inner journey from manipulation to actualization.* New York, NY: Abingdon.

Stanford, G. (1977). *Developing effective classroom groups.* New York, NY: Hart.

Stokes, J.P., & Tait, R.C. (1979). *Group facilitator training package.* Silver Spring, MD: National Drug Abuse Center for Training and Development.

Sugar, M. (1982, April). The adolescent in group therapy: Indications and technique. Presentation, Washington, D.C.

Weiner, M.F. (1984). *Techniques of group psychotherapy.* Washington, DC: American Psychiatric Press.

Yalom, I.D. (1985). *The theory and practice of group psychotherapy (3rd ed.).* New York, NY: Basic Books.

Yalom, I.D. (1983). *Inpatient group psychotherapy.* New York: Basic Books.

PART TWO

SAMPLE
MATERIALS

NOTES

SAMPLE 1: THOUGHTS FOR ADOLESCENTS AND OTHERS TO LIVE BY

1. Shame on your parents for the way you are today, but shame on you if you stay that way.

2. When you point the finger, three come back.

3. If it is to be, it is up to me.

4. You can win all the battles and lose the war.

5. It is better to be a live chicken than a dead duck.

6. Life's not fair.

7. There are no rights, without responsibility.

8. "Freedom is just another word for nothing left to lose."

9. Without dreams, there is no need to work. Without work, there is no need to dream.

10. The Golden Rule: He who has the gold, makes the rules.

11. Luck—the harder I work, the more I get.

12. All good things come to those who wait, if you work hard while you are waiting.

13. Use the talents you possess: for the woods would be very silent if no birds sang except the best.

14. The secret of happy living is not to do what you like but like what you do.

15. "When you lose your dreams, you'll lose your mind".

16. You can't run away from your problems because they always travel with you.

17. Everyone should be a turtle. A turtle only makes progress when it sticks it's neck out. It has a tough enough shell to take it when things go bad, and slow and steady it won the race.

18. How many psychologists does it take to change a lightbulb? One, but the lightbulb has to want to change.

19. (Insight) x (Action) = (Growth)

20. Judge people more by their actions than their words.

21. Praise is what you say to yourself after someone compliments you on what you have said or done.

22. The proof of the pudding is in the eating.

23. Nobody said it was going to be easy.

24. Proper prior planning prevents pitifully poor performance.

25. You learn when you listen, not when you talk.

26. Speak slowly, softly, and less often.

27. Shallow brooks are noisy.

28. You never get ahead by putting someone else down.

29. Good relationship—not the absence of conflict but the ability to resolve it.

30. A friend is someone who tells you what you need to hear, not what you want to hear.

31. "Why am I afraid to tell you who I am?", 'cause that's all I've got, and you may not like it.

32. Parents: give your children two things: (1) roots and (2) wings.

33. There are no jokes.

34. Counseling is a process, not an event.

35. When the mind is ready, a teacher appears.

36. Life is a mountain, not a beach.

SAMPLE 2: LETTER OF INVITATION TO PARENTS—FIRST YEAR

Pleasants County Middle School

Donna Pratt Barksdale, principal

C. David Graham, assistant principal

P.O. Box 469, Belmont, WV 26134

September 17, 1985

Dear

This year the Pleasants County school system is expanding its counseling services to include a group counseling program at the middle school. The aim of this program is to help students enhance their self-esteem, improve interpersonal skills, and learn self-responsibility so as to better achieve in the classroom setting. Our staff has selected students they believe would benefit from participation in this group experience as well as those who could contribute to the effectiveness of the total program. Eventually we would hope to see group counseling become a part of every student's curriculum.

Group counseling has unique strengths due to the significance of peer interaction during the adolescent years. It is a method of helping adolescents become more comfortable with and receptive to those around them. By talking, listening, and sharing various concerns that arise in their daily experiences at school, adolescents find new ways of coping with the stresses of growing up. Topics at the weekly group meetings may center around social interaction, classroom activities, feelings, and/or other areas of common interest and concern the group members may express.

Your child is invited to join one of several counseling groups to be held during the school day at PCMS. A meeting with parents will be held on Wednesday, September 25 at 7:00 p.m. in the PCMS auditorium to further discuss details of the program. At that time, administrative personnel, counselors, and teachers who will be involved with groups will be available to discuss specifics of the program and the benefits that you and your child may derive from participating.

Please return the attached note in the enclosed envelope to inform us of your interest in this program. If you have questions, please feel free to contact me. I look forward to seeing you on Wednesday evening.

Sincerely,

Donna Pratt Barksdale

DPB/sh

SAMPLE 3: CONSENT FORM SENT TO PARENTS

```
                    PLEASANTS COUNTY SCHOOLS
                    GROUP COUNSELING PROGRAM

                    PARENTAL PERMISSION


                              Date:  September 25, 1985


I give my permission for _____ to participate

in the group counseling program at Pleasants County Middle School

for the 1985-86 school term.



                         _____

                              Parents signature
```

SAMPLE 4: LETTER OF INVITATION TO PARENTS—SECOND YEAR

Pleasants County Middle School

Donna Pratt Barksdale, principal

C. David Graham, assistant principal

P.O. Box 469, Belmont, WV 26134

Dear

You've probably read and/or heard about the group counseling program which was instituted last year at PCMS. Staff, students, and parents believe the program was successful, and we have decided to expand the program for this coming year.

The goals of the group counseling program are to help students enhance their self-esteem, improve interpersonal skills, and increase self-responsibility so that students can better achieve in the class-room. Group counseling has unique strengths due to the significance of peer interaction during the adolescent years. By talking, listening, and sharing various concerns that arise in their daily experiences at school, adolescents find new ways of coping with the stresses of grow-ing up; they become more comfortable with and receptive to those around them.

Many students have indicated a desire to be a part of this program. The staff at PCMS has also nominated students that they believe would contribute to the effectiveness of the total program and could benefit from participation. We are requesting that you return the bottom portion of this letter, granting permission for your child to participate in group, in the enclosed envelope.

We will have a meeting of parents whose children are participating in the group program. That meeting will be held in mid-September; we'll let you know when a date's been set. If you have questions before that time, please feel free to contact me.

Sincerely,

Donna Pratt Barksdale

Donna Pratt Barksdale

I give my permission for _____ to participate in

the group counseling program at Pleasants County Middle School

for the 1986-87 school term.

_____

Parents signature

SAMPLE 5: LETTER TO PARENTS—SPRING PRIOR TO FIRST YEAR

Dr. John Barilla
Principal

Nicholas Sham
Assistant Principal

BANGOR AREA SENIOR HIGH SCHOOL
R.D. 2   Bangor, Pennsylvania 18013-9654

Phone: (215) 588-2105

Mrs. Kathryn Schott
Guidance Counselor

Mrs. Betty Miller
Guidance Counselor

Dear Parents,

Growing up is a difficult task for adolescents in today's society. Our youth face serious issues of drug and alcohol abuse, depression and suicide, divorce and remarriage of parents, peer pressure, alienation, disillusionment, poor self-concept and self-esteem, and teen pregnancy to mention a few. As adolescents strive for responsible adulthood, they face and struggle with real pressures.

We in the Bangor School District recognize the issues facing our students and invite you to a meeting on the topic of adolescents on Thursday, March 19, 1987. Dr. Fred Krieg, clinical child psychologist from West Virginia and special consultant to the Bangor Area School District, will present "ADOLESCENCE: THE DILEMMA OF ASPIRATION" beginning at 7:30 p.m. in the auditorium of the Bangor Senior High School. He also will discuss the Adolescent Group Counseling Program, which our School Board unanimously approved in February. Dr. Krieg will organize and supervise this program beginning in September, 1987, in our junior and senior high schools.

Since receiving his Ph.D. in school psychology from Ohio State University in 1973, Dr. Krieg has taught at the graduate level at numerous colleges and universities. He entered private practice in 1975. In 1981 he assumed the responsibilities of Treatment Coordinator of the Adolescent Mental Health Unit of St. Joseph's Hospital, Parkersburg, West Virginia. He is a member of the American Psychological Association, past-president of the West Virginia Psychological Association, and former chairperson of the West Virginia Council of Interprofessional Affairs. He pioneered the Pleasants County Project, in the highly acclaimed and successful group counseling program.

We are extremely pleased to have Dr. Krieg share his talent, skill, and expertise on the topic of adolescence with us. We hope that you will join us at the valuable and informational meeting on Thursday, March 19. Your help and cooperation are needed to make this program effective.

Sincerely,

John Barilla

Dr. John Barilla
Principal

SAMPLE 6: LETTER OF INVITATION TO PARENTS—
MAY EVALUATION MEETING

Pleasants County Middle School

Donna Pratt Barksdale, principal

C. David Graham, assistant principal

P.O. Box 469, Belmont, WV 26134

May 12, 1986

As you know, your child has been participating in a group counseling program this year at PCMS. We have had many positive comments from staff, students, and parents regarding the program. We have also had several inquiries from other schools who hope to replicate the program.

At the parent meeting held in September, several parents suggested a follow-up meeting to be held in the spring. Dr. Fred Krieg, who has been providing training for our staff, will be here to meet with parents on Thursday, May 22 at 7:00 in the auditorium. Counselors and teachers who have been working with groups will also be present.

We plan to continue and expand the program for next year, and we are interested in your thoughts and feelings regarding its benefits. I sincerely hope that you will be able to attend the meeting.

Sincerely,

Donna Pratt Barksdale

DPB/sh

NOTES

SAMPLE 7: LETTER TO PARENTS—FALL PRE-PROGRAM EVALUATION

WASHINGTON JUNIOR HIGH SCHOOL
Office of the Principal
1203 PLUM STREET
PARKERSBURG, W.VA. 26101

John Timothy Swarr
Principal

William C. Butler
Assistant Principal

TO: Parents of Group Counseling Students

FROM: Tim Swarr *J.S.*

DATE: October 23, 1986

SUBJECT: Burk's Scale

    Attached you will find a copy of the Burk's Behavior
Rating Scale. Those of you who attended the September
meeting with Dr. Krieg will remember being told that we would
ask you to fill out a questionnaire about your child. The
purpose of this is to help us in evaluating the effectiveness
of the group counseling program. Please complete the scale
and return it to the school as soon as possible. If you have
questions, please call.

SAMPLE 8: LETTER TO PARENTS—SPRING, POST-PROGRAM EVALUATION

WASHINGTON JUNIOR HIGH SCHOOL
Office of the Principal
1203 PLUM STREET
PARKERSBURG, W.VA. 26101

John Timothy Swarr
Principal

William C. Butler
Assistant Principal

May 8, 1987

Dear

    We are interested in determining the effectiveness of
the group program in which your child has been participating
this year. Last fall you completed a Burk's Behavior Rating
Scale. We are asking that you complete the same Scale again
so that we can compare some pre-post data.

    We're pleased with the response we've had to the program
from students and parents. We hope you share our enthusiasm!

    If you have questions, please call (420-9655).
Otherwise, we'd appreciate your returning the completed Scale
by May 15. Thanks for your help.

Sincerely,

Tim Swarr

jm

SAMPLE 9: PARENTING WORKSHOP FLYER

Parenting Workshop

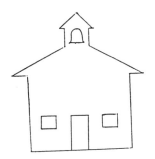

We all know that rearing happy, responsible children is a challenge. This series of five monthly parenting workshops is designed to provide assistance and support. The workshops will be conducted free of charge by Dr. Fred J. Krieg, a practicing child psychologist from Parkersburg, and Mrs. Diane Braun, Pleasants County Middle School counselor.

Location - Pleasants County Middle School Auditorium
Session 1 Date - Tuesday, January 20, 1987
Time - 7:00-8:30

Session 1: WHO SAID GROWING UP IS EASY?

-Effects of media exposure on children
   (TV, movies, music, role models)
-Future shock and megatrends
-Effects of an information (computer)
 society on children growing up
-Difficult decisions in difficult times
-Peer pressures, parent pressures

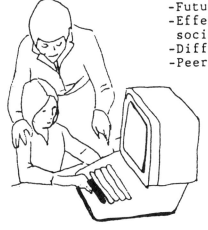

Child care services for children age 3 and older will be provided free of charge. The PCMS pool will be open with a lifeguard on duty. Students may watch videotapes, read, or do homework in the Media Center.

Session 2 February 17 - Promoting Self-Esteem
Session 3 March 17   - Thoughts for Adolescents & Others to Live By
Session 4 April 21   - Let's Not Forget Discipline
Session 5 May 19   - Issues That Face Our Youngsters

NOTES

SAMPLE 10: OFFICE LETTER OF INVITATION FOR GROUP PARTICIPATION

Fred Jay Krieg, Ph.D.
& Associates

Fred Jay Krieg, Ph.D
Martha H. McCoy, Ph.D
Candace E. Gardner, M.Ed
Eldon A. Frank, M.Ed
David J. Smith, M.A.
Richard E. Stanley

Grand Plaza
1107 9th Street
Vienna, WV 26105
(304) 295-9391

Medical Centre
202 Main Street
Ripley, WV 25271
(304) 372-3777

DATE

Dear Parents:

I will start a psychotherapy group in my office on DATE. The aim of this group is to resolve emotional difficulties, to improve interpersonal skills, and to encourage personal growth by having the participants share feelings, ideas, and concerns. It is my opinion that CHILD'S NAME will benefit from this type of group and also have a positive effect on the other members. I am writing this letter to inform you as to what I think are reasonable expectations from this experience.

Group psychotherapy with adolescents has unique strengths due to the intensified significance of peer interaction during the adolescent period. It is a method of helping adolescents become more comfortable and receptive to those around them. In the group, a child is less likely to feel isolated and alone because other members may offer moral support; objective criticism and/or useful alternatives to problem situations. Group psychotherapy helps adolescents make changes in themselves and their lives. It is an attempt to improve self-concept and self-responsibility as well as to develop better interpersonal skills. The method involves the adolescents talking as freely as possible, not only about worries or fears, but also about hopes and successes. The role of the group leader is to help the adolescent uncover underlying conflicts, deal with feelings and find new ways of coping with the stresses of growing up.

The reasons to do therapy in a group rather than on an individual basis are listed below:

1. The other group members are helpful. They are having problems too. Many times it is easier for an adolescent to believe or accept suggestions from other adolescents. It is also beneficial to have more than one person's opinion.

2. Adolescents learn about themselves by listening to others who have similar problems. It is comforting to know that they are not alone in their situation.

3. By talking in a group, adolescents learn the effects of their behavior on others and are made aware of their strengths and their weaknesses. The other group members present a mirror of that child's behavior and this increases the learning experinece.

-2-

4. When an adolescent is able to share experiences with peers, this allows for closeness, support, and increases the comfort level of the adolescent who tends to see themselves as more different than alike.

5. Group therapy becomes a place to practice the changes the adolescent makes before facing the actual situation. Group serves as a microcosm of real-life situations giving a secure, trusting, and friendly place to practice new behaviors.

The group will meet on every DAY from TIME in the group room in my office. It will be limited to eight members. I will serve as the leader and NAME will serve as co-leader. The room is large enough for all to sit comfortably in chairs in a circle where we can see and talk with each other. Basic rules for these sessions will be designed to protect the confidentiality of each group member. In the group, members are free to speak whenever they desire, remain silent, or redirect each other. There are no specific topics for this group but the discussion will generate from problems or situations the members wish to discuss. Everyone will be encouraged to respond to what is said. For those adolescents who have never experienced group, they may feel somewhat apprehensive and uneasy when they first enter group, but eventually they will be able to develop an interest and trust and will find group a very positive, enriching experience. In CHILD'S NAME, I hope you will see a gradual relief from stress, the development of self-assuredness, a greater ability to make decisions, and an increased comfort in relationships with others. I know these changes will take some time but they will, I think, occur through the group process; however, there are no guarantees. It is my feeling that group therapy represents a very positive experience for those who wish to put forth the effort to participate in the process.

The cost is thirty dollars ($30.00) per group session and payment is requested at the time of the session. Payments may be made in advance and our receipts will indicate credit on account. It is requested that a three-month commitment be made to attend group. It is my feeling that this commitment would enhance group attendance, which is essential for the group to be of maximum therapeutic value. Because many health insurance policies cover the cost of outpatient group psychotherapy, it is important to check your coverage. It is my hope that this group will meet for the remainder of the school year.

Please telephone the office by DAY, DATE, to confirm CHILD'S NAME participation in the group. If you desire further information or if I can answer any questions, please do not hesitate to contact me at my office.

Sincerely,

Fred Jay Krieg, Ph.D.
Clinical Psychologist
Group Leader

FJK/kg

SAMPLE 11: SCRIPT FOR INDIVIDUAL INTERVIEW

SCRIPT—INDIVIDUAL INTERVIEW

Introduce yourself and tell them who your secondary leader will be. Welcome them to group. You hope they will learn and enjoy things we will do. Talk about worries, fears, weaknesses, hopes, successes, school problems. One of our goals is to help each other with our feelings, find new ways of coping with being a teenager, at home, school, and with friends.

Why we do this in a group setting

1. All students have some problems

2. Teenagers listen to each other

3. Teenagers learn from each other

4. Students in the group will learn to help each other

5. Group will also give us a trusting, secure place to talk

What we hope to accomplish for all members in group (our goals)

1. Improve self concept, feel better about self

2. Become more responsible

3. Improve our interpersonal skills, learn to get along better

Membership in the group

All kinds of students, shy, talkers, those with problems, those without many problems. Tell them how many will be in the group (8, 9, or 10)

Where group will meet:

_____ room

Meeting Times

Every Tuesday during _____ period. Students will be excused from their classes and you will help them work out a schedule if they need to go into a class during their study hall. They should **tell you** if they have any problems with a teacher or with make-up work.

Room Arrangements

The room will be set up in a circle, go in and have a seat but do not sit in mine or the secondary leader's seats. They will be marked reserved. **Notes** will be on seats later. (Explain notes)

Video Taped Sessions

The camera will not be aimed at the group members, but at the leader and secondary leader. Reasons for taping—so that supervisor can help the leaders do a better job. Explain who supervisor is and why he/she is working with the project. Tell them that the only people who will be seeing the tapes will be supervisor and the **leaders from all the groups.** Mention that our purpose is not to evaluate the students but to help the leaders and secondary leaders learn to lead group more effectively and do a better job. Tapes are destroyed at the end of each month; after the supervisory session.

Rules of group—**IMPORTANT**

1. Confidentiality, "What is said in group, stays in group." We do not mention anything that is said in group to anyone else. (You might tell your parents what you say but don't tell them what other people are saying). This is hard but we must do it. If members can't be trusted, the kids won't talk. If someone breaks the rule they have to deal with the **group** and **me.**

2. Don't leave group without permission

3. One person talks at a time. You do not have to raise your hand, but you will take turns. Members are free to talk at any time or remain silent. No one is forced to talk.

Discuss Rules

Can you live with the rules? (Make them commit to the rules.) Do you have any questions about the rules?

Welcome Group Members

Welcome them to group, you are glad to have them and you will see them on **(date).**

SAMPLE 12: SCRIPT FOR RAPP—LONG VERSION

SCRIPT—RAPP—LONG VERSION

Please note that throughout this script there will be sections containing phrasing suggestions for you to use in your first few group sessions. These will be denoted by quotation marks.

Although the project model does not use planned activities, we have found that group is most successfully begun by using the Dyad technique as an activity to introduce group members to each other. This, and an activity we do at Christmas, plus a termination activity are the only activities we do in the thirty group sessions.

The First Group Session

The **Dyad Technique** is an activity in which each of the members spend three to five minutes interviewing each other. In a group made of ten individuals, you will break them into five pairs of two. They will interview each other, with the stated goal being to introduce the person they just interviewed. The primary leader and the secondary leader introduce each other to the group. In this manner you will have each of the group members introduced. You will find that each group member will do a more extensive job introducing someone else than if they introduced themselves. This activity serves as an icebreaker and gets things going in the group. It reduces anxiety and gives everyone the opportunity to talk in the first group and to find out something about each other.

The good group leader will also use the Dyad Technique to demonstrate that it is much easier to talk about facts than it is to talk about feelings. You will note that most of the information generated in the Dyad Technique is factual and not about how members are feeling, i.e., anxious or nervous. It becomes a good time for the group leader to show how much easier it is to talk about facts than it is to talk about feelings. This technique is a good way to generate discussion. The overall activity should take approximately half of the group time that you have allotted. There is a tremendous benefit, especially if you can get the discussion going, to talk about how hard it is to discuss your feelings. Do not cut it off at any point, but play it for everything you can get. Of note is the fact that if you go through the entire first group and actually never get to do RAPP that is okay. You can always do it in the next group. Much is gained in anxiety reduction if you get the group members to talk. When it is over, if you still have a little time left, you can do "R", the rules and then elaborate on it in the next week.

Therefore at the end of the first group, you have successfully completed the Dyad Technique and gotten through the beginning of RAPP, at least through the rules, having everyone agree to those rules. In the second session the minimum that you should do is to have everyone repeat the names of all the group members. Go around and have everyone introduce each other so that the names are learned. Explain the camera and then try to continue with the explanation of RAPP.

The next immediate issue to discuss is the camera. An important aspect for each student to understand is that the camera is on the leader for supervisory purposes, as a way of teaching. Just as the kids are learning about group, you are learning to lead groups. Explain to them that the tapes are reviewed only by the group leaders and the supervisor, who offer ideas to improve your skills as a group leader, and to improve the group. You will each have one tape; after four sessions, the supervisor will come in to review the tape. Explain that then you will erase and record over it. Go through any questions they have about the tape and the camera. Be sure to tell them that the camera will help you become a better group leader plus helping them become a better group. Assure them that no one but you, the other group leaders, and the AGCS consultant will ever see these tapes; not the principal, their parents, or their friends.

The Second Group Session

The following are the minimum things you must do in the second group session: (1) have everybody know the names of all the other members, (2) have everybody understand the camera, and (3) go through RAPP as best you can.

RAPP

In the second group session the group leader will be as active as he or she will ever be. You establish the procedures, rules, and rationale for group. You are teaching the students what group is all about. You want to tell them what you are going to tell them, then tell them, and finally, tell them what you told them. In other words, teach, reteach, and review. Indicate to them that you hope group will be a positive experience and help them grow as people. Tell the students what group is about and help them understand how they all relate to one another. Tell them that teenagers listen to each other better than they do anyone else and that this is an opportunity to share feedback. We hope they will feel less isolated and alone and that they can help each other. Tell them that they all have some of the same problems, and will be able to help each other with those problems. Students can offer alternatives to problem situations, learn their strengths and weaknesses, and become more comfortable with each other. They will learn to share and learn from each other. Remember that the group members are rather anxious; this is a threatening situation for them. They want to make a good impression on the members and the group leader. They do not have a concept of what group is about in terms of their own personal roles, roles of others, and leaders. They are distrustful and scared and they may be angry about being in group. This is important to recognize and remember throughout the first few group sessions.

You need to recognize that as a leader a perfectly normal situation is for you to be anxious and nervous. You know the importance of getting started properly and the pressure to do so makes you scared. Recognize, however that you are the only one who knows what a good group really is.

R—Rules

Rule 1. Now you are ready to review the rules. Remember, in each individual interview you went through the rules with everyone involved in your group. Now in your first or second group session, you will go through the rules again, starting by saying, "Does anyone remember the rules I discussed with you when we met individually?" Hopefully, one of them will come up with the rules. If not, you might start out yourself by saying, "The most important rule in group is *'What's said in group stays in group.'*" "Why would this be important?" "We give ourselves trust because it is essential and we need to respect that quality in a person and this is what group is about." Stress how important trust is, that being able to trust a person could be the highest compliment that we could pay them. "That is what the rule of confidentiality is all about. If we know what is said here stays here, we can be more open and honest with each other. That is very important."

One rule under confidentiality is that we will not talk about someone who is not here. On the day a group member is absent, you will not talk about them, what they have done, or what happened to them.

Rule 2. *One person talks at a time.* You might say to them, "Does anybody remember the second rule? Why do you think that rule is important?" "We each have ideas, thoughts, and feelings that we might want to share. But if we are talking, we cannot be listening. When one person talks at a time, we can benefit from what is being said. We can take turns appropriately, listening to what we have to say."

Rule 3. "Does anyone remember the third rule? *It is no one leaves group without permission.* We only have one group session per week. There will be times when you might feel like leaving because someone might say something you do not want to hear. It will be necessary for you to take these comments and learn from them. Even if you are uncomfortable, you need to stay. 'You can't run away from your problems because they always travel with you.' That is what group is about."

You might then say to them, "Do we all have the rules and understand them? Can you live by these rules? It is very important that everyone accept the fact that living by the rules is one of the most important things we can do."

At that point, remember that everyone must verbally or at least by head nod agree to live by the rules.

A—Approach

It is safe to say that the most difficult part to describe to group members is the "approach". Emphasize the "here and now" approach. This is best explained in Yalom's book **THE THEORY AND PRACTICE OF GROUP PSYCHOTHERAPY,** Chapter 5. Staying in the here and now all the time is probably an unrealistic expectation. To be much more realistic hope that you will be able to do it at least 50% of the time, so don't get upset if your group members talk about things that happened last week or last year. Remember to try to shift them from **what they say** to **how they feel** about it.

The approach or focus of the group is to talk about how we feel and how we feel about what happens to us. Talking about the "here and now" is a difficult concept, so you might say to them, for example, "I don't know about how you are feeling, but right now I feel kind of nervous. It is really kind of scary to me to be in group." "When I went through the training this summer, in the workshop, Dr. Krieg told us we would be very anxious the first time, and he was right. I do feel very anxious. When I started to talk I felt that butterflies might come out of my mouth. Anyone else have that feeling?" As they nod or shake their heads, you should say, "That is what we mean when we talk about a "here and now" feeling. We talk about how we feel at the time and then spend some time understanding that. I think the feeling of being nervous or anxious when you first come to group is a very normal feeling, but the fact that we realize that everyone feels that way kind of helps us feel less anxious. The more we talk about our problems, we find out that we are much more alike than we are different: the more comfortable we are going to be with this group process."

Some times a group member will come in and tell the group something that may have occurred over the weekend. Maybe a brother and sister got into an argument, or someone might still be upset about what Mom and Dad did. The important thing is how they feel about what happened, how they reacted, and how they handled their anger. Feelings are much more important than telling the actual events that caused it. "Learning to understand how and why we feel the way we do is an important part of what group is all about." "It is very important in life to learn to talk out our feelings; feelings toward parents, siblings, teachers, and friends." You might also tell them "Lots of times we have feelings that are very justified. We cannot change the situation but we can change how we react to it." Here you might tell them the story of the two boys who were on a beach, when a wave came in and it knocked the two boys down. One got up, laughed and waited for the next wave. The other boy got up, and ran to his mother calling 'Mommy, Mommy, the wave knocked me down.' "Was it the wave that made each boy act differently? It wasn't that the wave was good for one boy and bad for another, it was the reaction the boys had to the wave that made a difference. That is what we are talking about in terms of feelings." The feelings a person has regarding a situation are what is important. You can choose to act one way or the other. One of the things that we will accomplish in group, is to help each other be better able to talk about our feelings. Students may get very angry when they see a math paper with a low grade, especially one with a lower grade than anticipated. Yet, dealing with the anger can be as important as the grade itself. "How you deal with anger can make you feel better about yourself, or make you even more angry with yourself. It can lead to constructive or destructive work in school. Anger held inside you can build up and then all of a sudden, kind of explode. Keeping your feelings inside can be detrimental to you in the long run."

Remember that the group becomes a mini-example of the outside world; what happens in the group is probably an example of what would happen outside. If a child has problems getting angry in group, the odds are he or she has problems getting angry outside of group also; however, group is a safe, protected environment where you can learn how to handle that anger much more appropriately. "In group, you really don't have to tell me what your problems are, because I will be able to observe them myself. My job will be to help the group focus on communication patterns, getting along better, the immediate feelings of the members, and helping you build relationships that are positive." The leader's job is to create the environment of the group and to help process what is taking place within the group. "Always remember however, that it is your group and that what you get out of this group will be a function of how hard you work. There will be no activities in this group. This is your group and not mine or Mr. X's (co-leader). What you do with group and how much you get out of it is up to you."

(Please note that this part is explained almost exclusively by narrative example.)

P—Purpose

The students may wonder why they are here. "None of us are perfect. We all need improvement in learning to understand ourselves and how we feel about ourselves. To talk about what we think is easy, however to talk about how we feel is very difficult. In group we will have three major goals. Goal One (1) is to work on improving our self-concept. Do you know what we mean by self-concept?" (Throw that open to the group. Have them explain to you what it is.) "We want to improve our self-concept; that is, how we feel about ourselves. Some days we feel good about ourselves and other days we don't feel so good. How I feel about myself can have a lot to do with many things. In fact, there have been many studies that have shown how you feel about yourself has more to do with your success in school than even how smart you are. You all know how hard it is some times to take a compliment: someone will say

'Gee, you look nice today.' and you will get embarrassed or something of that nature. This is a function of a low self-concept." "It is hard for us to say thank you, knowing that the person really meant it. It is important to learn to feel better about ourselves."

Goal Two (2) is to improve responsibilities and accepting responsibility for our own behavior. "Each of us in our lives can become more responsible people. In what ways do you think you all could be more responsible?" (Let them give you a few examples.) "Yeah, I think you're right, like doing things on time, doing things correctly, getting your homework in, being dependable for others, being trustworthy. Being trusted by others is an important part of responsibility. Again, I want to stress to you the importance of the rules; people live by the rules, the rules of group are important. We have to learn to accept the consequences for our own behavior, so that if you get an F because you didn't study, it's good to be able to say that it was because you didn't study, not because the teacher didn't give you a square deal." "It is important to not play the 'blame game': this is an important part of being able to accept responsibility for our own behavior."

Goal Three (3) is to learn to get along with people better. "Everyone should want to improve skills in getting along with peers, friends, or adults. This is a very important skill, because how successful you will be in life has a lot to do with how well you will be able to get along with people. We spend a lot time as teachers, counselors, and parents talking about 'What do you want to be when you grow up?' Do you know that one of the most important skills that you can take with you on your job is the ability to get along with co-workers? This skill starts right here in school. If you don't learn it here, it gets harder to learn out on the work force. One of the things I hope you will get out of this group will be to learn to 'say what you mean and mean what you say'. Tell your friends what they need to hear, not just what they want to hear. Being able to say things directly to a person, in the long run, will make them better friends, plus make them respect you more. Those are the things I hope will come out of being in group. It is important to learn how your behavior affects others. Sometimes we don't realize how we interact with other people, and the affect of our behavior on others. It is a very positive thing to be able to tell someone how you feel inside."

(Please note: this whole section is entirely in narrative example.)

P—Phases

"Groups go through phases. What is a phase? It is like a stage of development: like a child who learns to walk or crawl. It is the things we observe in an individual as we go through time. Groups also go through certain stages. For example, right now we are all sizing each other up and kind of figuring out how we fit into the group. You are probably wondering what this is all about, and are really not sure, and are scared and distrustful. That is called the ***distrust stage.*** Time will be needed to get to the point where we are comfortable with each other: this distrust phase is a normal part of group. Group is a process and it takes time: anything worth doing takes time. To form a trusting group doesn't happen overnight. It will take some time for us to go through the phases in group until we get to the point that we are comfortable with each other. To form a group has a lot of similarities to meeting someone new. When you first meet someone, you don't tell them your deepest darkest secrets: what you tell them is a little bit to see how they handle it. The better you get to know them and find that they are trustworthy, and they care about you, the more of yourself you share. Group is like a series of friendships with a group of people. Time is needed before we trust each other, but gradually the more we see that everyone keeps the confidentiality rule and the other rules, then the more we will become a group. Remember this is your group, you determine if it is successful or not. How much you get out of it depends on how hard you are willing to work."

"I am very happy to be the leader. As leader, I have certain jobs I have to do. Today for example, I have talked and talked trying to teach you what group is about. The more group moves on, however, the less I am going to talk. This will move us into the ***integration stage.***" "In this stage, you will find that each time you come to group you will be more comfortable. Everyone of you will begin to make a contribution, some of you will talk a lot more than others, and some of you will listen better than others. I think you will begin to feel good about being here, about helping each other, and about being able to support each other. Remember what I said earlier, you won't always hear what you want to hear in group, but I think you will hear what you need to hear." "A friend is someone who tells you what you need to hear, not what you want to hear. We want to be honest with each other. Sometimes that takes some time to accomplish. So, as the group develops, we will get closer and closer and begin to work on the reasons we came to be a part of this group. Who can think of some things that we might end up talking about?" (Throw it open for ideas like problems that kids might come into, parents, or the 2.0 rule. If they happen to mention something that really isn't appropriate to talk about, you can "yes, we might talk about that, but I think we should talk about how we feel about that." It is important at this point for the secondary leader to be involved, in terms of providing some support—perhaps what he may hope to get out of the group.) "I would like to share one more thing: at no time will we—leader and co-leader—violate your confidence. I think the group will only be good if we obey the rules." "I want you to understand there are rules in the school that I need to live by. For example, if one of you tells me that you are going to hurt yourself or that you are a victim of child abuse or sexual abuse, then I am going to have to do something about that." "Also, I think that it is important that we live by the rules of the school in general. For example, you are not allowed to use bad language because it is not allowed in school. That is an important part of getting the group where we really want it to be."

"As the group develops, I hope that you will all get so close that you really want to help each other. When you do that, you will be in the ***working stage.*** The working stage means everyone will help and will be honest and direct with each other. You will begin to work on certain issues. At that point, you will be a cohesive group and you will feel really tight and close with each other and have a real desire to help each other. That is what the group is all about. As you get more comfortable, you will talk about things that are really important to you." "By the end of the year, we will have to end this group. This is called a ***termination stage.*** It will happen in May when school is ready to get out. I hope by then that you will feel sad that the group has come to a close. I hope this group will be as good an experience as it can be, and I hope that you will work to make it successful."

"Let me summarize what I have said here: groups go through stages, beginning with a ***distrust stage,*** then goes to an ***integration stage,*** then to a ***working stage,*** and then a ***termination*** or ***ending stage.*** Another thing which is very interesting is the fact that each group session ***recapitulates*** the phases that occur in the lifetime of the group." "Do you all know what I mean by recapitulates? What I mean is, that in the whole year from October through May the group will go through phases. Each session will also have a beginning, a middle, and an end." "The group will be much like the whole sequence that we will go through together. I will begin every group session by saying "what do you want to talk about today?" "That will get us started. With about 5 minutes to go, I will end each group session by saying "how did the group go and how did you do today?" "We will then go around and each person will say something. This will give us all a chance to talk, but it also will give us an opportunity to see what we learned in each group session. When you come into the group, I will have a summary sheet of each group session on your chair. You will be able to read them and review what happened last week. This will give you some ideas of what we might talk about in the group."

"When you come to the group you will be really worried about it but after awhile, you will get comfortable with the routine, because each group session will start the same way: the chairs will be in a circle, a summary sheet from the previous week will be on the chair, and you will have time to read them and see if things are in there that you might wish to discuss. We can discuss anything from the previous week that you want to before we move on with group. I want you to know that each week Mr. X (secondary leader) will collect those sheets and rip them up right in front of you. We will make sure that no one gets them."

"I sure talked a lot today, and threw a lot at you, but I want you to know that this is your group. Each week I will talk less and less, but I wanted to tell you what to expect and that I hope you like it." "Does anyone have any thoughts or feelings about what I have said?" (Use the extra time to wrap things up and put all that information together for them as best as possible. If you still have some time left, you might tell them some of the positive things that might happen in group. For example, gaining from common problems, giving information, sharing and supporting, learning to know ourselves better, and learning to become better, more intimate friends. Also, point out to them that the group is kind of like a club: they get to enjoy and support each other; learn to be open and honest with each other.)

The Third Group Session

In this session, when they come in, a summary sheet will be on each of their seats. On these sheets, you should have briefly written the rules. Mention in the sheet that the rules were agreed upon by everyone. You want to list and explain RAPP briefly. You might want to mention something about the camera, or highlight anything important that happened like people talked about being more responsible, or anything that might indicate positive things that members of the group said. The summary sheet is your support. After they have read through it, ask if they have any questions about it. Since they probably won't, pass them to your secondary leader, have the secondary leader rip them into pieces in front of the students, and then continue with the group session. Start by going over the rules in the group, have group members repeat them briefly just to refresh their memories. Talk about the "here and now", and the phases; all of this briefly. Then, find out what they thought about it all, ideas they might have, and their feelings about what went on. Don't forget that at the start of today's group after you are done with the summary sheets, say "what would you like to talk about today?" After you have finished briefly going over RAPP again to refresh their memories, you might ask some questions like, "what else? Are you feeling more comfortable today? Seems to me like everything is going pretty well. I've already seen some of the things I learned about this group this summer start to happen. I don't know about you, but the first time I was pretty scared. Now, however, I am a little more comfortable. Are you feeling that way, too?" Finish up by saying "how did group go and how did you do?" That will end the third group session.

NOTES

SAMPLE 13: SCRIPT FOR RAPP—SHORT VERSION

SCRIPT—RAPP—SHORT VERSION

R   Rules

A   Approach

P   Purpose

P   Phases

Reminder: Nothing is brought into the circle! No books, pencils, toys, etc. Also, I make them leave the arms on the chairs down.

Welcome everyone and have everyone (including leader and secondary leader) introduce themselves again (Dyad was done in first session). Tell the students that this is our _____ year with the group, and that they are part of a special group of kids who get to go to group.

RAPP—Rules, Approach, Purpose, Phases

RAPP teaches what group is about. We know that students listen to other students better than they do to anyone else and that this is an opportunity to share that kind of feedback. Everyone sitting in this group has some of the same problems and issues of growing up. We hope that you will

feel less isolated and alone,

offer alternatives to problem situations,

become very comfortable with each other and trust each other, and

learn to share and learn from each other.

R—RULES

(Review the rules.) Does anyone remember any of the rules I discussed with you when I met with you individually?

1. What's said in group stays in group. MOST IMPORTANT RULE and the hardest to abide by, but we must if we want everyone to trust us. Being able to trust someone could be the highest compliment that we could give.

2. One person talks at a time. Be polite and listen to what is being said.

3. No one leaves group without permission.

4. Remember that group is a class and that you need to act accordingly. You do not have to raise your hand, but proper "classroom behavior" is expected.

Does anyone have any questions about the rules? Can everyone live with these rules? (Make everyone commit to the rules either verbally or by nodding their head.) Remember, living by rules is one of the most important things we can learn to do.

A—APPROACH (The here and now)

This is your group and I want it to be your group. We can discuss anything you would like to discuss. Does anyone have any ideas about what we might talk about? (Try to generate a discussion. Opportunity for secondary leader to interact.) In the group my job is to create an environment for you to be able to talk safely, to help you learn to get along better, express your feelings, help you build positive relationships, but I want you to remember that what we discuss here is up to you and the group will be what you make it. You can talk about anything as long as it has something to do with how we are feeling, thinking, or problems we are having right now, our fears, worries, school, friends, families, or hopes, etc. We cannot talk about anyone who is not in group. If someone is absent or not a member of our group, we are not going to talk about him or her. The approach we are using is talking about ourselves in the "here and now", how we are feeling at the present time, how we react to situations, how we handle our anger, so we can learn how and why we feel the way we do. That is really an important part of our group, learning to talk about the way we feel and how better to handle our feelings.

P—PURPOSE

We are all here because none of us are perfect: we all need to improve on one or more of the three things we talked about when I met with you individually. The goals of this group or our purposes for being here are to improve in three major areas.

1. Improve *self-concept*—(Can someone define self-concept? Try to generate a discussion.) How I feel about myself. Some days we feel good about ourselves and other days we don't feel so great. It is important to learn to feel better about ourselves.

2. Become more *responsible*—What do you think we mean by being more responsible? (Doing things on time, doing them correctly, being dependable, being trusted by others, might even mention obeying group rules.) We also have to learn to accept the consequences for our own behavior, so that if we get and F, we accept the blame, not try to blame our teacher, for instance.

3. Learn to get *along better* with people—If you want to be successful in life, it is important that you learn to get along with people, whether it is your boss, your teachers or other authority figures. Those are people with whom you need to learn to get along.

P—PHASES

A group goes through phases as it develops. When you first meet a friend, you do not trust him with your deepest, darkest secret. You try out a little bit of information and see how he handles it. Then you work on trusting him more and more as he shows he is trustworthy. That is similar to how group works. Today everyone is a little uneasy, wondering what group is all about, and not trusting anyone else. This is very normal and is called the ***Distrust Stage.***

Then we will move into what is called the ***Integration Stage.*** In this stage we will feel a little more comfortable with each other, but you will find that we will be talking about safe topics; not really about ourselves, but about parents and teachers. We will begin to share some things that we all have in common, concerns or issues that we have.

We will acquire more depth in group discussions during the ***Working Stage.*** During this stage we will be working on what is important to you, your own personal issues, the issues of growing up. This is when you have learned to trust each other and have a sincere desire to help each other. Do you remember the things we discussed earlier that we might talk about: fears, worries, school, parents, friends? (Secondary leader can help here by suggesting topics to discuss or telling the group that adults are also here to help.) In the working stage is where everyone will try to help each other be honest and more direct with each other. Here you will learn that "a friend is someone who tells you what you need to hear, not what you want to hear." At this point, we will be trusting and caring enough of each other that we will be able to be honest with each other.

Unfortunately, group will end when school ends and we will enter the last phase, which is the ***Termination Phase.*** By then I hope you will be such close friends that you will be sad to leave group and that you will have valued the closeness and the experience of group. I hope all of you will understand as we go through these phases and help make the group successful.

Let me summarize what I have said: groups go through stages beginning with a distrust stage, then goes to an integration stage, then to a working stage, and finally a termination or ending stage. Another thing which is very interesting is the fact that each group session ***recapitulates*** the phases that occur in the year long lifetime of the group. What I mean is that each session will repeat (will go through) the four phases in one session, just as in the lifetime of the group. Each session will have a beginning, middle, and end. I will begin every group by saying "What do you want to talk about today?" and that will get us started and with about 5 minutes to go I will end each group by saying "How did group go and how did you do today?" We will then go around and each person will respond to that question by saying how they thought group went and how they thought group did. Are there any questions about that?

SUMMARY SHEET

You will note that when you come into the group each time I will have a summary sheet (notes) on your chair for you to read. (Discuss what the notes are for.) After you have read them, pass them to the secondary leader who will tear them up and destroy them, so that no one else can read them. This is another way we keep the confidentiality of the group.

VIDEO TAPE AND CAMERA

The last issue to discuss before we finish talking about what group is about is the video tape camera behind you. That video tape camera is there so my supervisor can supervise these groups. Does anyone remember why the camera is taping the groups? (Make sure they fully understand why the camera is in the room.) Are there any questions? Once again I would like to caution you about the importance of keeping the rules and that all of you did agree to do this. Time is up for today and we will pick up here next week.

SAMPLE 14: GROUP NOTES, NAME BY NAME FORMAT

GROUP NOTES

Group defined cliques, talked about fair weather friends, baby talking.

JOHN: Was feeling okay about the car accident. Told JEFF to tell the group how he feels about them. We all need friends to tell our problems to and keep out of trouble.

Kids use baby talk to cover embarrassment.

ROBERT: He is doing okay, but some kids still try to fight. Told JEFF that kids shouldn't leave the group and the group learns to treat them better. When older kids baby talk it doesn't set a good example and makes them appear very young.

TINA R.: Had trouble telling JEFF how she really felt about him. JEFF's father probably worries about his baby talking. Everyone needs a good friend, and she also has some problems with fair weather friends. Would like to talk more in group.

RICK: Still has some problems with the clique, but it is hard to leave them. Was very honest with JEFF even though it was hard—about his baby talking. JEFF probably needs a good friend.

TOM: Still having problems with the clique. Going to be nice to everybody to make friends. Embarrassed to talk.

TINA S.: STEVEN can show his old friends how not to fight. Baby talk makes us look immature.

BARBARA: Was absent.

JEFF: Admits to being in the clique, but is sort of afraid of some clique members, especially if they are in group. Admits to baby talking and that his father doesn't like it. Sometimes does it to get his friends to notice him. Complained about fair weather friends. Is going to work on the baby talking.

SHELLY: JEFF treats her okay in the halls.

Reminder—don't evaluate Miss Hart and her teaching. This is your group not hers.

"A friend is someone who tells you what you **need** to hear, not what you **want** to hear."

SAMPLE 15: GROUP NOTES, SUMMARY FORMAT

GROUP NOTES

The overall discussion in group today was about death, although the initial topic started out to be reincarnation. The group started talking about whether or not they believed in reincarnation, but **MIKE** was able to tell us that his grandfather died this summer. He was concerned about what happened to his grandfather and about what really happens to people after death. This led to some interesting revelations and sharing by group members.

DANA, VICKY, and **CHRIS** have a grandparent who died. **BECKY** and **PAULA** each have had close relatives who have died. **ERIC, JOE, TOM** and **ANGIE** have not had anyone close to them die. Group discussed how people handle death. You do not always have to cry immediately to feel sorry. **ANGIE** was able to point out that frequently at funerals people cry because they feel sorry for themselves. **MIKE** was able to talk about the fact that he got angry at his grandfather's funeral because he felt like his mother was not upset enough. That led to **DANA** talking about the fact that she doesn't really understand why people don't cry, because they feel better afterward.

Overall, the discussion was very intense. Group members seemed to be very willing to share their feelings and impressions. It was an excellent group and I hope we pick up on that discussion next week.

SAMPLE 16: ACTIVITY—CURATIVE FACTORS IN GROUPS

CURATIVE FACTORS IN GROUPS

Most people agree that participation in a group can help a person grow and learn about him/herself. The elements in a group that facilitate growth have been called curative factors. Below is a list of some possible curative factors in groups. Your task is to rank these factors in the order of their importance. Put a "1" beside the factor that you think is the most important in helping a person grow as a result of his/her group experience. Put a "2" beside the second most important and so on, until you have put a "10" beside the factor that you think is least important.

_____ Learning to give and receive feedback

_____ Group members thinking of themselves as a group

_____ Learning "why you do what you do" (insight)

_____ Receiving advice from other group members

_____ Finding out others have problems like yours

_____ Giving advice to group members

_____ Obtaining information

_____ Feeling comfortable in the group

_____ Getting support from others

_____ Ventilating feelings

NOTES

SAMPLE 17: DEVELOPMENTAL STAGE, GROUP BEHAVIOR, AND ITS EFFECT ON LEADERSHIP STYLE

Developmental Stage	Group Behavior	Leadership Style
Distrust (Session 1-6)	**P**articipation—Low **A**nxiety—High **R**esistance—High **C**ohesiveness—Low	Content to process Subjective (here and now) Group Empathy
Integration (Sessions 6-15)	**P**articipation—Moderate **A**nxiety—Moderate **R**esistance—High **C**ohesiveness—Developing	Process to content Subjective Group Empathy to clarification
Working (Session 15-27)	**P**articipation—High **A**nxiety—Low **R**esistance—Low **C**ohesiveness—High	Content Subjective (personal) Group and individual Confrontation (insight)
Termination (Sessions 27-30)	**P**articipation—High **A**nxiety—Moderate **R**esistance—Low **C**ohesiveness—Very High	Process Subjective Individual (taking the chair) Empathy and Confrontation (insight)

NOTES

FISHBOWL ACTIVITY

Participants: Choose to be one of the students in a heterogenous group of similar blending and composition to one of the project groups. Familiarize each other with the dynamics of each of your group members and then walk into the fish bowl in character. We will role play this group in each of the four phases of group.

Observers: Try to identify one group member for each of the roles listed below and record their name beside the appropriate description. Obviously, names will appear more than once as group members can play many roles in the course of a group.

Self-Oriented

Dominator
Recluse
Aggressive Blocker
Help Seeker
Recognition Seeker

Task-Oriented

Initiator
Information Seeker
Information Giver
Clarifier
Summarizer

Maintenance

Harmonizer
Gatekeeper
Encourager
Compromiser

Manipualtive

Placator
Blamer
Computer
Distractor

NOTES

SAMPLE 19: GROUP OBSERVATION CHECKLIST

GROUP OBSERVATION CHECKLIST

Group Leader — Primary
(Circle One)   Secondary

Grade level of Group _____

Week number _____

Date _____

1. Was the subject matter of the group discussion focused on the "here and now?"

1	2	3	4
no focus off task	some focus skipped from topic to topic	good focus "there and then" instead of "here and now"	good focus "here and now"

2. Was the discussion mainly factual or aimed mostly at group members' feelings?

1	2	3	4
all factual	mostly factual some feelings	equal amounts of factual and feelings	mostly feelings some factual

3. What was the level of participation in the group?

1	2	3	4
most members did not participate	less than half of the members participated	half of members participated	most members participated

4. Were members listening to each other and/or were ideas being acknowledged?

1	2	3	4
little or no listening in group	most did not listen well to others	average listening	most members listened well to each other

5. How open were the members sharing their own personal issues?

1	2	3	4
not open little productivity	able to verbalize but not on a personal level	willing to disclose on a personal level but superfically talking around the real issue	willing to self-disclose on a personal level

6. How comfortable are the group members?

1	2	3	4
high degree of uneasiness little to no eye contact fidgety	some uneasiness poor eye contact	relaxed good eye contact	open and comfortable able to sustain good eye contact

7. How much trust and openness is there in the group?

1	2	3	4
distrust	little trust	average trust	trust and acceptance
not accepting of each other	slightly defensive	some helpfulness	empathy demonstrated
	little concern for each other	some concern about fellow members	supportive of each other

8. What was the atmosphere of the group discussion?

1	2	3	4
defensive and inhibited	hostile and competitive	average cooperation	good cooperation
members afraid	signs of anger	some sharing	members value each other's contributions

9. Do members feel a sense of belonging to the group?

1	2	3	4
members have no sense of belonging	members not close but some friendly relationships	some warm sense of belonging	strong sense of belonging among the members
		friendships developing	

10. Who do the group members look at when talking?

1	2	3	4
leader only	mostly leader	equally between peers and leader	mostly peers
	sometimes peers		sometimes leaders

ADDITIONAL COMMENTS:

SAMPLE 20: ACTIVITY—EFFECTIVE USE OF SELF-DISCLOSURE

EFFECTIVE USE OF SELF-DISCLOSURE

Indicate where the following self-disclosures are **Beneficial (B)** or **Harmful (H)** to the growth of the group.

_____ 1. Feelings of anxiety about leading the group in the very first group session.

_____ 2. Doubts about competence as a group leader.

_____ 3. Anger at a specific group member.

_____ 4. An argument with spouse the night before.

_____ 5. Feelings that group is being non-productive.

_____ 6. Special feelings of affection toward a specific group member.

_____ 7. My own personal difficulty telling someone I care for that I like him/her.

_____ 8. Anger at the principal for scheduling an assembly on the day of group.

_____ 9. My use of marijuana as a college student.

_____ 10. Uncertainty about what is taking place in group during that group session.

_____ 11. Similar problems I had with my parents when I was their age.

_____ 12. Feeling pleased with the progress of the group.

NOTES

PART THREE

SUPERVISION

NOTES

SUPERVISION

Learning to be an effective group leader is an apprentice-ship trade. The many complexities and subtleties that arise in each and every meeting of a group requires that the group leader have a theoretical framework from which to operate, as well as competent ongoing supervision.

Using the core curriculum presented in the **Group Leadership Training and Supervision Manual,** group leaders learn a positive, practical model of highly tested techniques for promoting growth and change in adolescent groups. Through the knowledge gained in the training sessions, group leaders learn a frame of reference which assimilates what transpires within the group. Even when a group leader is experienced (educated and well-schooled), what a particular group will do during any stage of group development is unknown. The intervention strategies pre-sented during the training program help the group leader structure and operationalize the group through appropriate developmental stages. In order to accomplish that task, a necessary step is for the leader to master the information contained in this training manual. However, the cornerstone of the **Adolescent Group Counseling in Schools** program is the supervision process.

Supervision offers the opportunity to realistically appraise personal skills, strengths, and weaknesses, and is intended for those genuinely interested in achieving a higher level of group leadership effectiveness.

The supervisory process has two basic goals. The first is didactic in nature, whereas the second is designed to help the novice group leader feel more secure and confident. Both these objectives are met simultaneously with greater or lesser emphasis depending on the knowledge, experience and confidence of the trainee and the particular style of the supervisor.

The primary objective is didactic; to teach fundamental clinical methods and procedures. Effective group leadership requires knowing the essential principles of group dynamics. Supervision is not limited to teaching technique, but offers the opportunity to learn and understand group process. Leaders are taught observational skills and how to mold a group into a therapeutic system. Supervisory sessions provide the best avenue to insure that techniques and theory are consistent, and applied appropriately.

Helping the trainee become a more mature and confident individual is the second major objective of supervision. Initially, all novice group leaders are apprehensive. The role of the supervisor is to be supportive, and to guide each trainee without being too overprotective or controlling. The supervisor acts as mentor, trusted friend and counselor, shares experiences, and provides proper perspective to the learning process. Besides transmitting knowledge, the supervisor monitors the group's progress and facilitates the learning process. Ultimately, the supervisor must assess and evaluate whether the trainee has adequately mastered the information well enough to function independently as a group leader.

An additional role of the supervisor in the **Adolescent Group Counseling in Schools** project is to provide administrative support and intervention. To insure successful and smooth inclusion of group into each school's scheduling, the supervisor must encourage administrator, faculty, parent, and student willingness to participate. The faculty needs to be flexible in releasing students, providing make-up work, and, in general, be supportive of student participation in the program. Building principals must be willing to make every effort to prevent the scheduling of school-wide events (assemblies, field trips, tests, etc) on group days and/or during group periods. The supervisor needs to be available to assist and perhaps intervene in problems that may arise during the course of the year. This availability and support provide security for the trainees and are essential if they are to focus their efforts on learning effective group leadership skills.

Methods of providing group supervision are numerous, and all can be effective. At least one group should be observed entirely through its developmental stages, as opposed to observing varying or different groups. Observation can take on at least three forms: (1) video-tape; (2) one-way mirror; or (3) observing a group from outside the group with no interaction with it (Yalom, 1985). Observation should be followed by a post-group discussion as close to the end of the group session as is logistically possible. During this time, the supervisor should focus on three questions:

1. What did you like about what you did?

2. If you could do it again, what would you do differently?

3. What help do you need from me?

In the **Adolescent Group Counseling in Schools** project, participants are required to lead one or more weekly groups. A video tape of each of these groups is brought to the supervisory session where the leaders have the opportunity to submit them for peer evaluation and feedback. Supervision consists of meeting and conferring with other group leaders on a regularly scheduled basis to affirm growth and positive experiences, share common problems encountered, improve competencies, and provide peer support. The supervisory program enables the group leader to grow as the group is developing. Then, when the group is ready to deal with important issues, the leader is competent to cope with even the most difficult of group situations.

Conducted in this manner, supervision helps the group leaders develop a sense of unity which enables them to better serve students and each other. The process increases commitment to this cooperative enterprise. The role of the supervisor is to enhance this working together, while at the same time fostering self-learning and self-discovery. Participants are not involved in any personal process groups, rather the emphasis of this supervisory program is to maximize group leadership skills and become clinically proficient in the various elements of group dynamics. Supervision provides a structure for the trainee to look candidly, constructively, and reflectively at personal performance and ability.

Thus the **Adolescent Group Counseling in Schools** project consists of two key elements: training and ongoing supervision. Both are essential to successful adolescent group leadership.

ANNOTATED BIBLIOGRAPHY
ON SUPERVISION

1. Alonso, A. (1985). *The Quiet Profession.* New York: MacMillan.

   This book is totally devoted to the process of supervision of the group therapist.

2. Corey, G., & Corey, M.S. (1987). *Groups, Process and Practice,* 3rd Edition. Monterey, CA: Brooks/Cole

   Chapter 2, "Ethical and Professional Guidelines for Group Leaders," is essential reading.

3. Yalom, I.D. (1985). *The Theory and Practice of Group Psychotherapy,* 3rd Edition. New York: Basic Books.

   Chapter 17, "Training the Group Therapist," is the best overview of the essentials of the supervision process.

PROFESSIONAL ORGANIZATIONS INVOLVED IN GROUP TRAINING

1. American Group Psychotherapy Association
   25 East 21st Street, 6th Floor
   New York, NY   10010

2. American Psychological Association
   Division of Psychotherapy (#29)
   Section on Theory and Practice of Group Psychotherapy
   215 West 88th Street
   New York, NY 10024

3. American Association for Counseling and Development
   Association for Specialist in Group Work
   5999 Stevenson Avenue
   Alexandria, VA 22304

4. National Association of Social Workers
   7981 Eastern Avenue
   Silver Springs, MD 20910

5. American Orthopsychiatric Association
   19 West 44th Street, Suite 1616
   New York, NY 10036

SUPERVISORY SESSION #1
RAPP

I. RECORDING SECRETARY

A. Appoint Recording Secretary

    1. Takes notes

    2. Coordinator—distribute within one week, copies to supervisor, AGCS consultant, and all primary and secondary leaders.

    3. Notes

        a. Information

        b. Student concerns (no names)

        c. Reminders

II. OUTLINE OF SUPERVISORY SESSIONS

A. External Group Issues

    1. Administrative

        a. Principal, faculty, etc.

        b. Camera, room, etc.

    2. Coordinators and Leaders

        a. Forms due in/out

        b. Next supervisory date

        c. Any "housekeeping" items

    3. Student

        a. Death or terminal illness in family, etc.

        b. DUI, arrests, etc.

        c. Any pertinent family circumstances

B. Internal Group Issues

    1. Developmental

        a. Is group on schedule?

        b. What's keeping group from being on schedule?

2. Leader/Secondary leader

   a. Anxiety over process

   b. Group notes

   c. "Goodness of fit," okay?

3. Student

   a. Management

   b. Keeping rules

   c. Chronic lateness or absenteeism

C. Review Video Tapes of Groups

1. Procedure (during supervision)

   a. Tape should be at the exact place to be viewed

   b. Don't waste time hunting for "right spot"

2. Procedure (between supervisory sessions)

   a. Look for

      (1) Emerging leadership style

      (2) Ways to "head-off" problems

      (3) Leader/Secondary leader interaction

      (4) Subtle "clues" from group members

   b. Beneficial for primary and secondary leader to view tape together, if possible

D. Teach Next Stage

III. EXTERNAL ISSUES

A. Group Composition Forms

1. List of group leaders and secondary leaders

2. List of each group make-up

   a. Give leaders class schedule of each child

   b. Location of groups

B. Location of Groups

C. Camera and Microphone

    1. Leader knows how to operate camera

D. Leaders Each Have a Tape

E. Next Meeting Time

F. Concerns, Issues, and Problems

IV. INTERNAL ISSUES

A. Leaders—Any Concerns about the Make-up of Their Group

B. Individual Interview

    1. See script

    2. Remind students if they have a problem with classwork to tell you (if you cannot solve it, inform building coordinator or principal if necessary)

        a. Always better if handled teacher to teacher than if handled by "powers that be"

    3. Any scheduling problems

C. Primary and Secondary Group Leader Responsibilities

    1. Group summary

        a. Responsibility of primary leader

        b. Get to coordinator before group session

        c. System for distribution

    2. Group observation checklist

        a. Date *or* week number

        b. Copy of both to coordinator

V. FIRST GROUP

A. Place Reserved Signs on Primary and Secondary Leaders' Seats

B. When Entering Group Make Sure Members Do Not Have Anything in the Group; all books, pencils, etc. are outside the circle.

    1. Arms down on chairs

    2. No gum or candy

C. Dyad Technique (See p. 60 in Section One and Figure 4.)

    1. Good ice breaker—anxiety reducer

D. See Instructions p. 60, B. 3

    1. Allow 10 minutes for each pair to interview each other

    2. Pair students as illustrated in Figure 4.

Primary leader

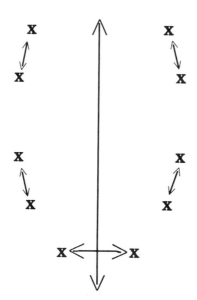

Secondary leader

Figure 4. Positioning for dyad technique (x = student).

    a. Leaders introduce each other

    b. If nine members, secondary leader pairs with a student and primary leader introduces him or herself

E. PROCESS (See p. 60, B. 2)

    1. Lead them to realize that it is easier to talk about facts than feelings

    2. Take as much time and generate as much discussion as possible

    3. If less than ten minutes left, stretch out until the end of the period

F. If 15 Minutes Remains, Start RAPP and Get Through the Rules Section

G. End Group by Saying, "Today we got to know each other and to feel more comfortable with each other. We will continue next week."

H. Summary Notes Should Contain Brief Information on Each Child's Interview Plus Whatever Was Said in Remaining Time; e.g., it is harder to talk about feelings than facts.

VI. SECOND GROUP SESSION

A. Prior to Group, Review Long RAPP Script (See Sample 12 in Sample Material Section of this book)

B. Place Summary Sheet on Chair of Each Member, no summary sheet on leaders' chairs

C. Short RAPP Can Be Taken into Group (See Sample 13)

   1. Cover in as much time as you like

   2. Goal of group is to get members to talk

      a. Any place a discussion is generated—keep it going

      b. Finish RAPP later

   3. At a minimum, cover Rules then "go with the flow"

D. Rules

   1. Every child must agree individually and in front of everyone to live by the rules

   2. Document on the summary sheet

   3. Remind them that group is a class and they are to act accordingly

      a. Do not have to raise hand

      b. Proper "classroom" behavior

E. Approach

   1. "This is your group and I want it to be your group"

   2. Does anyone have any ideas about what we might talk about?

      a. Try to generate discussion

      b. Opportunity for secondary leaders to interact

   3. Primary and secondary leaders should look for commonalities among group members

      a. e.g., "I notice most of your parents are divorced"

      b. Try to show that you have an interest in them and know something about them

      c. However, do not single out any one child or be too specific

   4. Next—explain "here and now" approach

      a. See the "Approach" section in Samples 12 and 13

b. Remind them that we do not talk about anyone who is not in the room (group)

   (1) Absent member

   (2) Someone in the school

   (3) Parents

c. To stay in the "here and now" 100% of the time is impossible.

   (1) Must obtain enough history to understand what generated the feeling being discussed.

F. Purpose

   1. Follow "questioning" approach in attempt to generate discussion

      a. e.g., What do we mean by self-concept?

   2. Purpose to build better social skills

   3. Groups follow good teaching practice—teach—practice—feedback

G. Phases

   1. Most children will not understand or care about this portion of RAPP

   2. Therefore, best to follow the friendship analogy

   3. Distrust phase

      a. Share nervousness

      b. Give opportunity for secondary leader to get involved

      c. Try to generate discussion about the members' anxiety and apprehension

   4. Integration phase

      a. Key word here is SAFE, e.g., parents, teachers

   5. Working phase

      a. Talk about things that are really important to you—"your own personal issues"

      b. You will learn—"a friend is someone who tells you what you need to hear, not what you want to hear"

   6. Termination phase

   a. This is not important to group members now

   b. Go over quickly, just telling them that group will end when school ends in May

H. Other Aspects of RAPP

   1. Recapitulates

      a. This it the time you first introduce the opening and closing statements

      b. Students will be alerted because it is the first time you have told them they will have to speak in each group

   2. Do not open group with "What do you want to talk about today?" until you are actually ready to turn group over to them

      a. RAPP has been completed and reviewed

      b. See Figure 5 for summary of content of initial group sessions

   3. Do not close group with "How did group go and how did you do?" until you have completed RAPP and reviewed, and have had some discussion after

      a. See Figure 5 for summary of content of initial group sessions

I. Summary Sheet

   1. By now, they have already seen the summary sheets

   2. Review process of destroying the summary sheets stressing the confidentiality issue

J. Camera

   1. Has been on throughout each session

   2. Again, stress purpose of camera and how tapes are re-recorded over to emphasize confidentiality

K. Reminders

   1. Old leaders be careful not to be too confident and imply that you know it all and know what will happen next

   2. No need to go around the group to summarize at the end of first group

      a. Ask if everyone understands and can live by the rules

      b. If you did not finish RAPP, then say, "We'll pick it up from here next week"

      c. If you finish RAPP, just ask if everyone understands and can live by the rules and you'll see them next week

VII. THIRD GROUP SESSION

A. See the preceding Section VI, Second Group Session

B. Summaries are on the chair; summary should contain

   1. If RAPP has been completed

      a. Condense RAPP from sheet

      b. Whatever else has been discussed

   2. If RAPP has not been completed

      a. Condense RAPP from sheet only as far as the group has completed

         (1) Be sure the rules are listed and everyone's agreement is documented

      b. Whatever else has been discussed

   3. Emphasize disposal of summary sheets and confidentiality

      a. Also can discuss tapes and how they are handled

C. After Summaries are Collected Begin Group by Having Members Summarize RAPP as Far as You Have Gone to Date

   1. Use good teaching techniques

      a. Avoid question and answer

         (1) Try to generate discussion

      b. Don't call on anybody by name

      c. Don't make anyone answer

      d. Avoid going around the circle in order

   2. Treat just like a class discussion

      a. Helps group members relax, they are used to acting in this manner in school

      b. Who remembers the rules?

      c. What is group about?

      d. What are our goals?

      e. Does anyone remember the stages of group?

D. If You Completed RAPP in Group 2

    1. Then summarize as above, and then generate discussion using questions below

        a. Are you more comfortable today than the first time?

        b. Are you less nervous this week?

        c. How are you feeling about group?

        d. Is it what you expected?

        2. End group by asking how group went and how they did

E. If You Did Not Complete RAPP in Group 2

    1. Summarize as above

    2. Complete RAPP

    3. Generate discussion

    4. Do not close by going around the group

    5. Close by saying good group, etc

    6. Do not go around the group until you have completely reviewed RAPP

F. Secondary Leader Needs to be Verbal and Assist Primary Leader in These Discussions

VIII. FOURTH GROUP SESSION

A. If RAPP Has Been Completed and Reviewed and Some Discussion Took Place in Third Group Session,

   1. Summary sheets are on chairs

   2. Any questions about summary

   3. Pass to secondary leader who destroys them

   4. What do you want to talk about today?

      a. Look down

      b. Do not wait too long

      c. Use questions of last session (VII.D.1.a. thru d.)

      d. Try anything to generate discussion

      e. If that does not work, use hook

   5. Hook—Did I mislead you?

      a. Is this what you thought group would be like?

      b. The counter-dependent group member (the angry, resistant hostile member) will use this lead to turn his/her anger at the group leader by indicating that this is not what he/she thought group would be like

      c. Group leader **does not** get defensive but rather

         (1) Turns the discussion to the group

            (a) Is that the way you all see it?

            (b) Did the rest of you hear it that way?

         (2) Look to your model to start the discussion

      d. The anger and resistance (the "meat" of group) will then be used to generate a discussion

B. If RAPP Has Been Completed in Session 3 But Not reviewed

   1. Summary on chair

   2. Any questions about summary

   3. Pass to secondary leader who destroys them

   4. Review RAPP as per Section VII. C.

   5. Then generate discussion as per Section VII. D., E., F.

   6. Group 5 will then start as Section VIII. A.

GROUP NUMBER	FASTEST CASE	SLOWEST CASE	WRITTEN SUMMARY	OPENING STATEMENT	CLOSING STATEMENT
FIRST	DYAD PROCESS	DYAD PROCESS PARTIAL RAPP	NO	NO	NO
SECOND	RAPP	PARTIAL RAPP	YES	NO	NO
THIRD	REVIEW RAPP BEGIN DISCUSSION	FINISH RAPP	YES	NO	YES IN FASTEST NO IN SLOWEST
FOURTH	BEGIN DISCUSSION	REVIEW RAPP BEGIN DISCUSSION	YES	YES IN FASTEST NO IN SLOWEST	YES

Figure 5. Summary of content of initial group sessions.

SUPERVISORY SESSION #2
DISTRUST PHASE

I. EXTERNAL GROUP ISSUES

A. Administrative

    1. Faculty Cooperation

        a. Students' work

        b. Coverage

        c. Leaders need to "run interference" for students in group

        d. Best way to solve a problem is for the group leader to speak with fellow teachers

    2. Schedule

    3. Room

    4. Camera and microphone

B. Coordinators

    1. Administrative

        a. Recording secretary doing job

        b. Summaries and checklists turned into coordinator

            (1) Coordinators keep file on each of them

        c. Supervision summaries need to be sent as soon as possible to AGCS consultant

        d. Group leaders' list to AGCS consultant

        e. Group members' list to AGCS consultant

    2. Student issues

        a. Any additions or deletions from group

            (1) Have other group members explain RAPP to new member

            (2) Do not do termination activity, it is too soon

C. Evaluation

    1. Distribution of Burks' Behavior Rating Scale

2. Parent—Coordinator's responsibility

   a. See cover letter (Sample 7, Letter to Parents, in Sample Materials Section of this book)

   b. Mail with return envelope

   c. Do not let student deliver

   d. Give students a number, not by name

   e. Student assistants can score

3. Teacher—Secondary group leader's responsibility

   a. Keep list of who you gave it to

   b. Remember to choose someone who will have the student for an entire year

   c. Be persistent

   d. If teacher is resistant and asks why

      (1) Burks' is a way to find out if the program does what it says it does

4. Score and obtain profile—return to coordinator.

5. Do in October

II. INTERNAL GROUP ISSUES

A. Developmental

   1. Attendance, tardiness

B. Primary/Secondary Leader

   1. Make sure to make contact with every group member every group

      a. Non-verbal and/or verbal

      b. Talk to "both sides" of the group

   2. If either leader is not able to be present for a group session, be sure to let coordinator know

      a. Group will be led by one person sitting in primary leader chair

      b. Coordinator can assist, e.g., "rounding up" students

   3. Secondary leader

      a. Verbal during this stage (sessions 3-6)

      b. Be the primary leader's rudder

      c. Be the primary leader's eyes and ears

      d. Primary and secondary leaders watch your own tape together

         (1) Give feedback

         (2) Review what is taking place in the group

         (3) Review individual members

         (4) Make sure you are working together as a team

      e. If you do not have time to review the tape

(1) Make a chart of the group (Figure 6)

Primary Leader

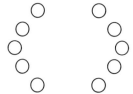

Secondary Leader

Figure 6. Chart of seating arrangement in group.

(2) Repeat above (d.) using the chart

C. Summaries

1. First names of students (last initial if necessary)

2. Mention everyone

3. Be vague rather than specific

4. Do not include anything that is not said in the group

5. If student has a reading problem

    a. Read it to him before group (the day before)

    b. In group the student will pretend to read it

    c. If many students cannot read—begin group by reading summary

D. Students

III. REVIEW VIDEO-TAPES OF GROUP SESSIONS

IV. TEACH DISTRUST STAGE

A. Leadership Style

1. Process

    a. Modeling

        (1) Communication skills

        (2) Listening skills

    b. Teach members how to relate to each other

2. Subjective

    a. Fearful, anxious

    b. Can disclose these feelings

        (1) Good modeling

        (2) Decreases tension

    c. "Here and now" disclosures only

    d. Uneasiness with first group regardless of experience

    e. Universality

        (1) "This is my first group, too, and I'm pretty scared."

3. Group

    a. Focus on constructing the group

    b. Leader dependent

    c. Will lose group if focus shifts to any one individual

        (1) If you help one, the others will become fearful of bringing up something for fear the whole group will focus on them

        (2) How do the rest of you feel about that?

        (3) Does anyone else have that problem (concern)?

    d. If issue is important, see that student individually

        (1) "I am concerned about what you were saying in group."

(2) "We did not have enough time to discuss your situation"

(3) "Can I help you?"

4. Empathy

   a. Anxiety reduction

   b. Unconditional positive regard

   c. Avoid anger response

   d. Conflict must be avoided if at all possible

      (1) Throw it back to the group

B. Leader—Most Active

   1. Establish procedures and rules

   2. Create expectations for group

   3. Predict problem and feelings

      a. Validate their feelings

      b. "I know it's hard to talk now"

   4. "Set the stage"

      a. Share values

      b. Non-judgemental

      c. Okay to express feelings

      d. "Say what you mean and mean what you say"

   5. Teach how to give appropriate feedback

      a. Modeling

   6. "Therapeutic pause"—

      a. Give them enough time to express themselves

      b. When you are ready to say something—wait thirty (30) seconds

      c. Do not rush—the goal of group *now* is to have them talking on a feeling level in *Spring*

      d. Let the group do the work

         (1) Slow down

(2) Do not expect too much too quickly

(3) Allow them to talk about surface material

(4) Do not *force* "here and now" discussion

e. Often not responding is many times more powerful than responding

7. In groups 3-6, turn the group from yours to theirs

a. Let the group solve its own problems before you solve them

b. Secondary leaders talking will help shift the focus off the primary leader

8. "Lead the witness" (or playing dumb)

a. Could you tell me more

b. Could you be more specific

(1) I'm not sure I understand? Can you explain that to me?

(2) Can anybody help me understand?

9. Other interrogative statements which might help to move group along

C. Group Members' Behavior

   1. Participation—low

      (a) Members are strangers

      (b) Fear of losing control

         (1) Of saying too much too soon

      (c) May be angry at being there

   2. Anxiety—high

      (a) Threatening situation

      (b) Desire to make a good impression

      (c) Lack of clear understanding of what to expect

         (1) Use to teachers telling them what to do

         (2) Explain different role of group leader and teacher

         (3) "What do I do now?"

   3. Excitement

   4. Resistance—high

      (a) Distrustful

         (1) Leader

         (2) Each other

      (b) Hesitant to participate (fear of being "called on")

      (c) Anxiety

      (d) Test leader and each other

         (1) Will question the rules as a "test"

   5. Cohesiveness—low

      (a) Too early

      (b) Poor communication skills

      (c) Inadequate listening skills

         (1) Will learn as group develops

D. Other Thoughts About Group Members' Behavior

1. If you have a split in your group, e.g., boy/girl, quiet/verbal

    a. Try to draw in both groups

    b. Do not point out the split or get heavy handed

2. If the split is by economics (poor/affluent), there is nothing you can do about it

    a. Stay out of it

3. It is too early to correct group for not being in the here and now

    a. Just be glad they are talking

4. Groups that appear to be in the working stage at this point

    a. May have working stage topic but will not stay with it or delve deep enough yet

5. Watch body language and group positioning

    a. Will start to move physically "into" the group

    b. Members' eyes will "dance" checking out everyone's reactions

        (1) Will stop in November

6. Often what they do not say is as important as what they do say

    a. "My parents make me angry...." Another group member responds, "Who did we play on Friday night?"

NOTES

SUPERVISORY SESSION #3
INTEGRATION PHASE

I. EXTERNAL GROUP ISSUES

A. Administrative

B. Coordinators

    1. Summaries of each group

    2. Checklist from each group

    3. Summary of supervisory sessions

        a. Distribute as soon after session as possible

        b. Send a copy to AGCS consultant

C. Evaluation

    1. Progress to date

    2. Keep in your possession

II. INTERNAL GROUP ISSUES

A. Developmental

B. Leaders' Concerns and Issues

C. Student

III. REVIEW VIDEO-TAPES OF GROUPS

IV. TEACH INTEGRATION STAGE

A. Leadership Style

1. Process is major emphasis, but move toward content

   a. Less active

   b. Shape the group as a therapeutic system

   c. Reinforce group's content discussions when on task

   d. Actively facilitate processing of thoughts and feelings

      (1) Begin to move group from cognitive to affective material

   e. Shape norms through modeling

   f. Protect the process

2. Subjective

   a. Reinforce curative factors as they develop

   b. Self-disclose positive feelings as group increases in cohesiveness

3. Group

   a. Reflect antagonism back to the group

      (1) "Does everyone else feel that way?"

   b. Encourage and support member to member interaction

   c. Process advice giving

   d. Leader should avoid giving advice

   e. Do not focus on personal issues that surface

      (1) Choose horizontal over vertical interventions

   f. Help group become agent of change

4. Empathy

   a. Listen empathetically

   b. Clarify

   c. Summarize

   d. Stop just short of confrontation

B. Other Thoughts About Group Leadership

1. Now is the time to narrow the focus

2. Teach

   a. More appropriate group behavior

   b. More appropriate group topics

3. Time to say

   a. "What's that got to do with group?"

   b. "Let's not talk about someone who is not here."

   c. "Let's try to stay in the 'here and now.'"

4. Do not rush the process

   a. "Counseling is a process, not an event"

   b. Bridge analogy

5. Two biggest mistakes of beginning group leaders

   a. Talking too much

   b. Fighting for control

6. Lead without domineering

   a. More effective if members say to each other what they need to hear

   b. Leaders can say it and then get the members to repeat it or support it

      (1) This can effectively be done in the role of summarizing either during the group or at the end

   c. If a student supports leader when you are working on a problem

      (1) Show appreciation

      (2) Preferably non-verbally

      (3) Try to get others to "join the band wagon"

7. Try to get them to talk to each other

   a. Look at the floor

   b. Hand gestures

   c. "Don't tell me, tell ..."

8. Communicate to them that it is safe to share

   a. Your role is group leader, not teacher

   b. Okay to say whatever you want to say

   c. Focus on positive outcomes of situations that the group is working on

9. Helpful techniques

   a. Use clarifying statements

      (1) "It sounds like you are saying ..."

   b. Try to incorporate "sayings"

   c. Try to use analogies

      (1) "You can't hurt someone's feelings."

      (2) "No one can make you do anything."

      (3) "When you point the finger, three come back."

   d. Sample the group

      (1) Rating system (1-10)

      (2) Voting

         (a) Use to generalize discussion from just two people in the group to entire group

         (b) e.g., "No one likes me."

         (c) Only use when you know what the outcome will be

         (d) Good to use on someone who is "tough to reach"

   e. If a topic presents itself and you are not sure whether or not you should discuss it, **DON'T**

      (1) Can you get too heavy too soon?— **YES**

10. Be sure to take the child with you if you have something disclosed that needs to be handled by the coordinator

   a. e.g., Suicide

C. Secondary Leader

1. Both leader and co-leader are decreasing their activity level

2. Try to read what direction the leader wants to take and follow

3. Make insightful interjections when it is going slow to pull the group along and to keep enthusiasm going

D. Group Members' Behavior

    1. Participation—gradually increases

        a. Each group begins with silence

        b. Moves to safe topics

            (1) School issues

            (2) Activities

        c. Advice giving

    2. Anxiety—moderate

        a. Gradually decreases as trust develops

        b. Participation itself serves to decrease anxiety

    3. Resistance—high

        a. Individual resistance starts to decrease

        b. Group resistance remains high

            (1) Intra-group conflict begins

                (a) Impatient with each other

                (b) Impatient with the process

                (c) Frequently off-task

                (d) Change subject—non-relevant material

            (2) Transferred to leader

                (a) Silence

                (b) Private conversations

                (c) Subgroupings

                (d) Outside group contact

                (e) Direct hostility

                (f) Antagonism

                (g) Testing of leader

    4. Cohesiveness—developing

        a. Bonding begins

    b. Feelings expressed

        (1) Mostly negative

    c. Norms are developing

        (1) Listening

        (2) Improved communication skills

        (3) Learning to give feedback

        (4) Disclosing honestly

    d. Curative factors beginning

    e. Confidentiality no longer a major concern

    f. Less leader dependent

E. Other Thoughts About Group Members' Behavior

    1. Generally—topics should last longer and fewer issues should be discussed

    2. Topics will become more meaningful and more personal

    3. How groups avoid "working"

        a. Fight—verbal or physical

        b. Flight—change subject

        c. Dependency—look to group leader to save them

    4. If they do not take "wrap-up" seriously

        a. Their group not yours

        b. Why group is important

        c. Why we "wrap-up"

        d. What it means when we laugh when we should be serious

        e. If you don't think their responses in summarizing were appropriate

            (1) Repeat procedure

SUPERVISORY SESSION #4
CHRISTMAS ACTIVITY

I. EXTERNAL GROUP ISSUES

    A. Administrative

    B. Coordinators

    C. Group Leaders

II. INTERNAL GROUP ISSUES

    A. Developmental

    B. Leaders' Concerns and Issues

    C. Student

III. REVIEW VIDEO TAPES OF GROUP SESSIONS

IV. TEACH CHRISTMAS ACTIVITY

A. Purpose

1. To make usually non-productive group productive

   a. Members' minds are on everything but group

      (1) Christmas parties, activities

      (2) Presents

2. Provides everyone the opportunity to participate in group prior to the Christmas break

   a. To express feelings

   b. To share feelings with each other

   c. Primes members for the working stage

3. Gives members the opportunity to generate therapeutic information for use in the working stage

4. Provides material to use for the group immediately following Christmas vacation

   a. Groups begin the Tuesday immediately following return from Christmas vacation and students have not yet settled into the "swing of things"

   b. Leaders may have little information about what happened to group members during the break

B. Procedure

1. In group immediately preceding the last group before Christmas vacation, e.g., (December 15 if last group is December 22), tell group—"we'll have a special activity for Christmas" next time .

   a. Do **not** tell them anything specific about the activity

   b. Sets the stage for a serious exercise

   c. Key to this activity being effective is for it to be spontaneous

2. Begin group by saying, "because it is Christmas, I think it would be nice if we did something special for this time of the year."

3. "Let's talk about Christmas wishes"

4. Everyone give a special Christmas wish for you and/or your family

   a. Something you want to happen or take place

   b. Must be realistic and honest

c. Cannot be a materialistic wish

5. At times a demonstration of what is expected may be necessary

   a. Primary and secondary leaders can demonstrate

   b. Decide ahead of the group which one of you will do this

   c. Try to choose a wish which is

      (1) personal

      (2) reveals something about yourself or your family you would like to see changed

         (a) e.g., "I would like to get along better with my brother or sister."

         (b) "I wish my mother and father would stop fighting and be more accepting of each other."

6. Then go around the room and let each child answer question 4

   a. Primary and secondary leaders decide ahead of time which group member will "volunteer" to go first

      (1) Pick someone who

         (a) is highly verbal

         (b) will give the type of response you desire

   b. Proceed to go clockwise or counterclockwise in order around the circle

      (1) Depending on which direction will give you more productive responses

      (2) Depending on which direction will give you more time to reach the most non-verbal member of the group

   c. Once you start, go around the circle in order

   d. Everyone **must** respond when it is his or her turn

      (1) Insist if you have to or even coach that person a little bit

   e. Encourage members to give honest and realistic wishes

   f. If you do not get the type of response desired,

      (1) Stop the process

      (2) Role model for them again

      (3) Start again

g. If the answer to the question is too general, (for example, if the member says something like, my wish is "peace on earth") then say "how about something that is a little more personal that relates to you more directly" and then have the person answer.

h. Primary and secondary leaders also respond with secondary leader going first

   (1) Can lengthen or shorten the time this activity takes to complete by the length of the comments made

   (2) Key is keeping the timing as appropriate as possible

   (3) Can use this time to emphasize, summarize, and highlight important "wishes" made by group members

      (a) e.g., "Bobby's wish to improve his grades is important and I hope he makes it a New Year's resolution to study hard and get his wish"

7. If, during the discussion, you hit on something that is of general interest to the group, follow that around and try to go into some depth on it. Do that as much as possible, remembering to make sure that every kid in the group should get to talk during this session

8. If time allows, repeat the exercise with the second question, "A special wish for someone else *in the group*"

9. In written summary, list individual members' wishes

C. First Group in January

1. Begin by saying, "What do you want to talk about today?"

   (a) If group begins a meaningful discussion, do not follow the procedure outline in this section

   (b) If group is silent, then ask, "Did any of you get your wishes for Christmas?"

2. This question attempts to tie the group preceding Christmas vacation with the group after Christmas vacation

   (a) The hope is to generate something meaningful to talk about.

   (b) Remember you have the summary which lists specific wishes; e.g., "I hope my brother comes home for the holidays."

   (c) You can ask, "Did your brother come home for the holidays?"

3. If this does not generate a meaningful discussion, a logical and productive procedure is to ask, "Did anyone make New Year's resolutions?"

   (a) Do not go around the room with this question

   (b) Return to good group leadership technique and "look at the floor"

NOTES

SUPERVISORY SESSION #5
WORKING PHASE

I. EXTERNAL GROUP ISSUES

    A. Administrative

    B. Coordinators

    C. Leaders

II. INTERNAL GROUP ISSUES

    A. Developmental

    B. Leaders Concerns and Issues

    C. Student

III. REVIEW VIDEO-TAPES OF GROUP SESSIONS

    A. Christmas Activity

    B. Integration Stage

IV. TEACH WORKING STAGE

A. Leadership Style

1. Content

   a. Encourage maximum group self-direction

   b. Use group to deal with underlying dynamics

   c. Educate and impart information

   d. Confront resistance

2. Subjective

   a. Can disclose personal issues if relevant

   b. Can be an "expert"

3. Individual and/or Group

   a. Therapeutic alliance established

   b. Can take greater risks

   c. Can intervene vertically if so desired

   d. Can make mistake and group will support and/or rescue

   e. Generate feelings and let the group do the work

   f. Identification among members allows individual work

      (1) "Going around the room technique"

      (2) Voting

   g. Focus on defenses

      (1) Denial

      (2) Displacement

      (3) Projection

   h. Provide insight and interpretation into underlying dynamics

   i. Allow group to be a place to practice new behaviors

4. Confrontation

   a. Generate feelings through confrontation

b. "Stir the pot"

c. Confront—material not the person

d. Differentiate between heavy focus and scapegoating

e. Confrontation is best done by group

　　(1) Second best by leader

f. If confrontation fails—go to empathy

g. Remember: The more confrontive the leader gets, and the more focus on the individual, the greater the risk

B. Other Thoughts About Group Leadership

1. Now is the time to "go for it"

a. You have worked to get to this point, now make it happen

2. Leaders can be as active and assertive as they choose to be

a. Fit your own personality

3. Model appropriate behavior

a. Operate on a feeling level

b. "A friend is someone who tells you what you need to hear, not what you want to hear"

4. Can work on an individual group member

a. Everyone knows and cares about everyone else in the group

b. Group will support you because they also want to help that group member

c. Individual counseling with a cheering section

5. When in doubt, throw it back to the group

a. "What do you all think?"

6. Remember each week's session will not be a working stage group

a. Usually do not pick up where they left off the week before

b. Individual resistance may increase

c. Group resistance may increase

d. Groups can scare themselves

7. Working stage behavior can lead to distrust

8. "The ego of the group is greater than the sum of its parts" (Thomas Marrone)

    a. Group will not let you go too far

    b. "Misbehavior" to accomplish that objective

9. Remember the leadership task, "To maintain control and provide protection"

10. Use judgment about spilling (talking to group leader outside the group)

    a. Turn it back to group if

       (1) It is about someone in the group

       (2) It is about group itself

       (3) It is a good topic for group to discuss

    b. Deal with it individually (and/or with your coordinator) if

       (1) Personal and "touchy"

       (2) Legal

11. ***Do not be so involved in content that you forget process***

C. Secondary Leader

    1. Secondary leaders can be more verbal and take a larger role than in the integration stage

       a. Avoid rivalry with primary leader

       b. Remember fantasy of group leaders being romantically involved

    2. Secondary leaders with aggressive primary leader need to be more involved than if primary leader is not aggressive

       a. To soften the primary leader

       b. To bail the primary leader out of problems arising from aggressive style

D. Group Member's Behavior

   1. Participation—high

      a. Less concerned about making good impression

      b. Feedback honest and constructive

         (1) "Friend is someone who tells you what you need to hear, not what you want to hear"

      c. Not afraid of losing control

      d. Roles established and comfortable

   2. Anxiety—low

      a. Safety in group

      b. Ready to self-disclose personal issues

   3. Resistance—low

      a. Group resistance is low

      b. Optimistic and positive about the group experience

      c. Individual resistance may be high as more personal and intimate material begins to surface

      d. Member may panic and want to quit the group

      e. Makes up excuses to be dissatisfied

         (1) Why did you say ...?

         (2) I don't like ...

      f. Why now?

         (1) Slow them down

      g. Move to group as a whole orientation

         (1) Process with the group

         (2) Help member feel less isolated

      h. Real issue—fear of intimacy and involvement

   4. Cohesiveness—very high

      a. Intimacy has developed

b. Curative factors at work

c. Members are interdependent

E. Other Thoughts About Group Members' Behavior

   1. Anger and resistance are the "meat" of the group process

   2. Anger in group is acceptable, not dangerous

      a. Everyone benefits from a group member's anger

      b. Relate to "real issue"

         (1) Feeling triangle

         (2) Defense mechanisms

   3. Be aware of scapegoating

      a. Make a definite distinction between constructive criticism and being cruel

      b. Point out reasons for scapegoating

   4. If seating position changes,

      a. Look for reasons

      b. Comment to the group about it

SUPERVISORY SESSION #6
SELECTED CASE REVIEW

I. EXTERNAL GROUP ISSUES

  A. Administrative

      1. Next year

         a. Summer training

         b. Numbers of groups

      2. Feedback Day—need dates

         a. Student assemblies

         b. Faculty meeting

         c. Parent night

  B. Coordinators

      1. Leaders for next year

      2. Students for next year

         a. Those who are in this year who need to be in next year

             (1) Our school

             (2) If new school next year (graduates)

         b. New students

         c. Obtain permission slips from students and parents

  C. Evaluation

      1. Post-program evaluation to be done after last group

         a. Teachers—obtain list of those who returned them in the Fall

         b. Parents—only sent home to those parents who returned them in the Fall

II. INTERNAL GROUP ISSUES

  A. Developmental

  B. Leaders' Concerns and Issues

  C. Students

III. REVIEW VIDEO TAPES OF GROUP SESSIONS

A. Review Selected Case Studies

IV. TEACHINGS

A. Group Leadership

1. Try to have everything that occurs in the group relate to the three original purposes of group

   a. Microcosm of the macrocosm

2. Try to make positive use of non-verbal disclosures of group members (facial gestures, off handed remarks)

   a. Direct it to the group member, e.g., "John did you have some concern about what Billy is saying?"

   b. e.g., "You don't believe him?"

3. Use of the "Hold Button"

   a. "What is going on in group right now?"

   b. Process the process

4. Transference and counter-transference

   a. Transference—the feelings that the group members have for and about the group leaders

      (1) May reflect feelings for or about significant others

      (2) "Trial run" on leader

         (a) Depending on how well it is handled by leader and group will determine if they try to resolve issue with the significant other

      (3) Transfer these feelings to group members

      (4) Definition of group cohesiveness

      (5) "The problem with transference is that it is only transference"

   b. Countertransference the feelings that the group leaders develop toward all or certain (may be just one) group members

      (1) May reflect personal issues

      (2) Normal, but non-productive, if not recognized and dealt with

         (a) Discuss it with co-leader in private, when you have time

B. Secondary Leader

    1. Avoid rivalry with leader

    2. Be as vocal as you choose to be

        a. "E.F. Hutton" of the group

C. Group Members' Behavior

    1. Group members want to connect with you, in spite of their behavior which may appear to the contrary

    2. "Does it appear that the group members feel group is satisfying?"

        a. "Are they comfortable?"

        b. "Do they enjoy group?"

        c. "Is group helpful?"

        d. Examine these issues of group members

            (1) Can be direct enough to ask a., b., or c.

    3. Is trust an issue?

        a. Is the group personal, intimate?

        b. Is the group open and honest?

        c. Are the group members interdependent?

    4. Are group members friends?

        a. Is the friendship diffused throughout the group?

        b. Are subgroupings the predominant structure?

    5. Are the group members willing to speak out, listen and respond to each other?

    6. Remember—the more emotional difficulties the group member has, the more basic the issue, the more primitive the defenses

NOTES

SUPERVISORY SESSION #7
TERMINATION PHASE

I. EXTERNAL GROUP ISSUES

    A. Administrative

        1. Next year

            a. Summer training

            b. Number of groups

        2. Feedback Day—need dates

            a. Student Assemblies

            b. Faculty meeting

            c. Parent Night

    B. Coordinators

        1. Leader for next year

        2. Students for next year

            a. Lists

            b. Permission slips

            c. Schedules

            d. Referral information on to next year's school (if applicable)

    C. Evaluation—Post Program

        1. Parents

        2. Teachers

        3. Students

II. INTERNAL GROUP ISSUES

    A. Developmental

    B. Leaders' Concerns and Issues

    C. Students

III. REVIEW VIDEO TAPES OF GROUP SESSIONS

    A. Review Selected Case Studies

IV. TEACH TERMINATION STAGE

    A. Termination Is As Important As The Beginning (RAPP). Just as in RAPP, the leader plays a crucial role in the termination process

    B. Termination Is Important Because

        1. It supplies a concrete ending to the group

        2. It summarizes the growth and demonstrates the progress that everyone has made

        3. It gives feedback to group members and also teaches them how much skill they have learned in being able to give feedback to others

        4. It is a way to say goodbye

        5. It creates motivation for those who will be in group next year, in the sense that they hope next year people will say nice things about them

            a. For the successful member, it is a positive experience and further motivates them

            b. For the less successful member, it hopefully increases the desire to do better next time

        6. It encourages the use of new skills and strengths. It is important to encourage them to continue to develop their interpersonal skills over the summer

    C. Group Members Will Come to the Termination Stage with Two Initial Feelings

        1. "I'm glad it's over"

        2. "I'm going to miss it (them)"

    D. Termination Is a Part of Life

        1. Everything has a beginning, a middle, and an end

E. Procedure

    1. At the time you review these notes, there will be at least three more group sessions

F. Third Session from the End

    1. It is important in the beginning of the termination stage to discuss next year. Begin to process with the group members in general terms what might be available next year, that some may be in group next year and some may not. It they are in group, it will most likely not be with the same leader, and definitely will not be with the same children

    2. Solicit names of members for next year

        a. Find out who wants to be in group next year and who does not

        b. You may do this in any manner you wish

            (1) Open discussion

            (2) "Going around the group technique"

    3. For those who are in the sixth or ninth grades, inform them whether or not there will be a group program at their new school

        a. In the event that they are to be selected for group next year in their new school, they will be notified

G. Second Session From the End

1. Try to generate a non-specific discussion about feelings, about group, progress made, etc.

2. The material that follows is a possible script for this session

    "We have been together for almost thirty weeks now. All of us have grown in some manner. I have observed your maturing and being more adult every day. Your interpersonal skills have improved, you are getting along with others better, and understand yourselves better. You have improved your problem solving skill and seem to take more responsibility for your own behavior. Some of you have made large strides in these areas, others have not done as much. I really believe we have all benefitted from group in many ways, including myself. We have all learned to share with each other and we have learned that we all have very similar attitudes and feelings. It was our goal in the beginning to get together and talk about our feelings; I think, in fact, that we have been able to do that fairly successfully. I think you all have developed a lot of new skills and I hope that you will use them." At this point I would pause and ask them, "How do you feel about leaving?" (PAUSE FOR ANSWERS); example, some of them will answer "I'm glad it's over", some will say "I am going to miss it (them)." Then you might add some things like:

    1. "Name some things about yourself that have changed this year."

    2. "What do you like or not like about group?"

    3. "I think you have all made some new friends here this year, good and caring friends, and I think that is important. You might want to keep in touch with those people over the summer, and as far as I am concerned it is perfectly okay if you want to trade phone numbers and addresses between this week and next."

    4. After the summary of this session, end by saying: "Next week we will be doing something special. It is an activity that we have developed to say goodbye to each other, to summarize our progress, and to tell each other how we feel about each other. It will be a chance to share the growth and progress we made."

H. Last Group Session—"Taking the Chair"

"TAKING THE CHAIR"

"Taking the chair" is a very important part of the termination process. It gives an end to the beginning, it gives everyone in the group an opportunity to express their feelings and to share their feelings with each other.

I think you will find out even the most negative things will come out in a positive manner during this process. I think you also will learn that you have accomplished much more than you are aware of. You will hear that in the feedback that each of the group members give each other, and also in the feedback that they give you. I think one of the purposes of "taking the chair" is to find out how much was accomplished and also to end on a very positive note.

PROCEDURE

An important procedure is for the leader and the secondary leader to decide ahead of time which member will **receive** comments first. (Pick someone whom you know will draw positive feedback from the group.) Also important is that you pick a member to start giving the feedback in the process. Here you want to pick someone who is highly verbal, and also someone who will make positive comments.

At times a demonstration may be necessary to show what we are talking about by having the leader use the secondary leader as the person who is receiving feedback and give feedback as an example. For example, "You have been a good co-leader, you have been very supportive and helpful, I think you have done a good job handling the summary sheets, and I really have valued having you in the group with me." That gives an example of some of the positive things. You might add something like "I kind of wished as a co-leader that you would have talked earlier, because I've noticed as this group has progressed you've talked more, and that's been very helpful to me and to the group."

Pick a target person to start the feedback process. That person again should be someone you know is verbal and will say positive things. You then have the choice to proceed either clockwise or counter-clockwise depending on who you feel will give you more positive information, or who will give you more time to get to someone who might give negative feedback, or who might be very withdrawn and/or nonverbal. It is important to note that once you start the pattern of the circle, you are locked into it. Do not go out of order, do not break the chain. If it comes up that the person you want to receive the feedback first is one seat or two seats away from the person you want to give it, then have two people go and then skip the person receiving the feedback and continue to stay in the same order.

Encourage group members to give honest and constructive comments to each other; if you don't get positive or beneficial feedback or members don't understand what you are asking of them, stop the process, role model again for them (it is important to teach them what you expect from them), and then go back and start over. The rules are the following:

1. The person receiving the feedback may not reply to anyone else's comment after the person says it. They must wait their turn until everyone, including the leaders, has given their feedback to make any kind of reply.

2. The members must talk **to** the person on the chair, not about that person. For example, you can't say, "John did pretty well," you must say "You did very well."

3. Everyone in the group must say something even if you have to wait or coach that person a little bit. Every person **must** talk when it is their turn. This may take some time but it is absolutely essential. You will find that even the most withdrawn member will say more and more as the process develops.

Leaders and secondary leaders need to give and receive feedback last after each of the group members has given their feedback, the secondary leader going first and the leader going last, before you move on to the next child. After all the children have gone around giving feedback, and before the secondary leader and leader give feedback, you should ask if anyone has anything else they would like to add before the leaders take their turn. Once the secondary leader and leader finish giving feedback that person is completed, then go to the next person.

The secondary leader and the leader are to receive feedback from the group members after the entire process of each of the group members is complete. I think you will find this to be very beneficial to discover what the group members have to say about each of you.

SOME IMPORTANT REMINDERS

Should for some reason the process go sour and the group members "gang up or dump" on one of the members, I remind you that one of the primary tasks of the group leader is to protect the group members; therefore, stop the process, reemphasize the difference between constructive criticism and being cruel, then proceed again with the process. You cannot allow the group to scapegoat one another.

Realize that this process may run over the allotted time, therefore if the process is running late, people must be available to cover your classes. Either the counselor, the school psychologist, or principal will be available to cover. If you see your group is running over, have the secondary leader go out quickly and notify the counselor so that arrangements can be made for class coverage.

Should "taking the chair" run over, a back-up room is necessary in order to accomodate the start of another group.

A key to making this entire process work is that it be spontaneous. For that reason, in the next to last session do not tell the members exactly what will happen. Both leader and secondary leader can lengthen or shorten the time it takes to complete this process by the length of the comments they make. They are the key in keeping the timing as appropriate as possible. However, do not cheat the group or yourself, this may be the most meaningful event of the year for group members and/or group leaders.

NOTES

ABOUT THE AUTHOR

FRED JAY KRIEG, Ph.D.

Dr. Krieg is a clinical child psychologist who has been in private practice since 1975, treating adults, adolescents, and children. He has taught on the graduate level at several colleges and universities, and has served as Treatment Coordinator, Adolescent Mental Health Unit, St. Joseph's Hospital of Parkersburg, WV. Before establishing his practice, Dr. Krieg was Director of Educational Services, Nelsonville Children's Center, Nelsonville, OH.; Assistant Professor of Education and Coordinator Developmental Disabilities Training Program, University of New Hampshire, Durham, NH.

In addition to his private practice, Dr. Krieg heads a consulting firm that specializes in promoting professional development in the area of group counseling. The *Group Leadership Training and Supervision Manual* (Accelerated Development, 1988) is Dr. Krieg's new book written about his consultation and supervision experience during the *Adolescent Group Counseling in Schools Project,* and serves as a basis for American Group Counseling Services, the consulting service that provides comprehensive group counseling programs in schools (presently servicing and operating in four states).

Dr. Krieg received his bachelor's degree at Boston University and his master's at the University of Massachusetts. Later degrees include a second master's at Ohio State University, and a Doctor of Optometry at Ohio State University in 1972. That same year he received the James A. Bing Memorial Award for Outstanding Research in Visual Perception, and in 1975 he was elected to Fellowship in the American Academy of Optometry. He earned his second doctorate at Ohio State University in school psychology with a major in learning and behavioral disorders and minor in mental retardation. Dr. Krieg is licensed to practice as both an optometrist and clinical psychologist.

Dr. Krieg is a member of the American Psychological Association and the American Group Psychotherapy Association. He is past-President of the West Virginia Psychological Association and formerly chairperson of the West Virginia Council on Interprofessional Affairs.

Dr. Krieg has published articles in several professional magazines and journals, and lectured throughout the United States. He is the author of:

KNOWING THE CHILD WITH SPECIAL NEEDS
(Head Start Technical Assistant and Management System, OCD, Chicago, IL, 1973) (3rd edition, Learning Workshops, Belpre, OH 1977)

HYPERACTIVITY: DIFFERENTIAL DIAGNOSIS AND TREATMENT
(Learning Workshops, Belpre, OH 1977)

SCREENING PRESCHOOL CHILDREN FOR HANDICAPPED CONDITIONS
(Learning Workshop, Belpre, OH 1978)

THE SCHOOL AGED CHILD WITH LEARNING AND BEHAVIORAL DISORDERS
(Educational Resource Services, Landsdale, PA 1980)

ADOLESCENT GROUP COUNSELING IN SCHOOLS
(Ohio Valley Press, Belpre, OH 1985)